THE FIRST GREAT
OCEAN LINERS
IN PHOTOGRAPHS

193 Views, 1897–1927

WILLIAM H. MILLER, JR.

With the Assistance of the Museum of the City of New York

DOVER PUBLICATIONS, INC.
New York

To My Grandmothers
with their love and patience, all things were possible

Published in Canada by General Publishing Company, Ltd., 30 Lesmill Road, Don Mills, Toronto, Ontario.
Published in the United Kingdom by Constable and Company, Ltd., 10 Orange Street, London WC2H 7EG.

The First Great Ocean Liners in Photographs: 193 Views, 1897–1927, is a new work, first published by Dover Publications, Inc., in 1984.

Book design by Carol Belanger Grafton

Manufactured in the United States of America
Dover Publications, Inc., 31 East 2nd Street, Mineola, N.Y. 11501

Library of Congress Cataloging in Publication Data

Miller, William H., 1948–
    The first great ocean liners in photographs.

    Includes index.
        1. Ocean liners—History—Pictorial works.   2. Ocean travel—History—Pictorial works.
I. Museum of the City of New York.   II. Title.
VM381.M446 1983   387.2'432'0222   83-5292
ISBN 0-486-24574-8

ACKNOWLEDGMENTS

Many hands have assisted in the compilation and completion of this volume. The author wishes to note the exceptional help of four masters of ocean-liner history and materials: Frank O. Braynard, Arnold Kludas, Richard K. Morse and Willie Tinnemeyer. Most important assistance, in photographs, material and inspiration, has also been provided by Erwin Abele, Frank Andrews, Ernest Arroyo, Marius Bar, Ken Young and the City Archives of Victoria, British Columbia, James Cooper, John Crowley, the Cunard Line, George Devol and the World Ocean & Cruise Society, Frank Duffy, Alex Duncan, Lori Fabiano, Captain James L. Fleishell, Herbert G. Frank, Jr., Rolf Finck, Erika Lisson and Hapag-Lloyd, F. W. Hawks, Anita Heimbruch, Doreen Heywood, Lucy Holland, Eric Johnson, Barry Kogan, Julie Ann Low, John Maxtone-Graham, Vincent Messina, Jennifer Bright, Nancy Kessler-Post and the Museum of the City of New York, Hisashi Noma, Ralph L. O'Hara, David E. Pettit, Donald V. Reardon, Charles Ira Sachs and the Oceanic Navigation Research Society, Richard Sandstrom, William Schell, Victor E. Scrivens, Roger Sherlock, Peter Smith, Steamship Historical Society of America, Robert Turner, the United States Lines, Everett Viez, and the World Ship Society Photo Collection. Of course, and hardly least, warmest thoughts and appreciation to my family for their inspiration.

SOURCES & PHOTOGRAPHERS

CONTENTS

FOREWORD

Since part of my family has lived for over a century in Hoboken, the New Jersey waterfront city that is just across the Hudson River from New York City, it has had a personal connection with some of the ships shown in these pages. Grandmother Miller was 11, a young girl out for a day's fun on her roller skates, on that Saturday afternoon in June 1900 when the city's German steamer piers burned. Nearly 75 years later she recalled that the sky was covered for miles in thick blankets of smoke. Some, especially the Italian residents, thought it was "the end of the world." Some terrified locals began to scatter from the site, clutching a few possessions. Grandmother told me of the sounds—a dramatic mixture of rattling fire trucks, bells, horns, whistles and those distant, horrifying screams of the German crewmen trapped aboard the burning liners.

Grandfather Miller once told me of spending hours waiting at the same piers, by then rebuilt after the fire, to tour the brand-new *Kronprinzessin Cecilie* in 1906. The chance to inspect the vast and luxurious innards of Imperial Germany's newest Atlantic greyhound was well worth the wait. He also recounted endless Saturdays when young men assisted at liner sailings, particularly at the 16th Street dock of the Lamport & Holt and Scandinavian-American lines, helping passengers with their baggage. On good days, they could earn as much as $2 for their efforts.

Of course, all of my early family members had vivid recollections of the war years along the Hoboken docks. At first, in 1914–15, the German liners sat, laid up and without life, looked after by loyalist crews and sometimes used by partisan groups for fund-raising parties for the "Kaiser's war." Such a collection of motionless ships, in their political limbo, was a reminder to Americans of that far-off war. Then, nine days after the United States entered the hostilities in 1917, in a dramatic step, that idle fleet and the German-owned piers were seized. Special police from outside Hoboken were brought in to watch over the site and even to close the German shops near the docks. The area became the port of embarkation for America's Expeditionary Forces—the immortal "doughboys." (A small memorial stone with a bronze plaque in commemoration still stands on River Street.)

Troopships, many of them former German liners, began sailing with large numbers of servicemen bound for the trenches of Europe, inspired by General Pershing's words, "heaven, hell or Hoboken by Christmas!" However, the process was not without its problems. First, the existing 237 Hoboken saloons were a fierce temptation to pier guards and troopship crews. They were quickly closed by official order for the duration of the war. Christmas boxes posed another dilemma. The Government suggested that it would be a nice gesture for the troops to receive a present from home for Christmas 1917. However, every box had to be inspected for bombs and other possible sinister contents before going overseas. At first, the local command posted six officers and 250 men to inspection duty. Within days, the arrival rate of packages grew to such an extent that 70 officers and 1160 men were needed.

At the war's end, Grandfather Miller, by then a local police officer, often had special duty along the docks as thousands cheered each homecoming troopship and as the transport trains traveled away from the pierside terminals. There were also those occasions of great sadness, silence and tears as trains passed out of the docks carrying the wounded and the dead. In 1919, there was yet another crowd-filled event. Schools were closed and children lined the streets, waving tiny American flags. Factories were shut and long blocks of River Street tenements were decorated in flags and banners. The occasion: President Wilson was arriving home, at the Third Street Pier, aboard the *George Washington*, having signed the Versailles Peace Treaty.

There are now few reminders along the Hoboken shore of those long-ago days of great liners and festive receptions, of midnight sailings and even of passenger service across the Atlantic. The red-brick bulkhead buildings remain which once housed the offices and reception for the North German Lloyd and Hamburg-America Line and where, in the north turret, the Lloyd's pier superintendent once had a canvas rooftop swimming pool. Center Pier B, which had welcomed the likes of the *Imperator* and *Vaterland*, the largest liners afloat in those fateful few years just before the start of the Great War, is also intact. But the entire facility, all but completely closed, has been used only for storage in recent years. Shipping has gone. Doors and windows are locked tight, the wind rattles through onetime passenger and cargo openings and the underdeck pilings are eroding slowly in the changing tides of the Hudson. Current plans are to demolish the complex and replace it with housing and office space.

These pages have been assembled for yet one more nostalgic tribute to a part of the great history of passenger shipping. Like the Hoboken docks, it now seems part of a very distant memory, of a very different way of life.

WILLIAM H. MILLER

Hoboken, New Jersey
Christmas 1983

INTRODUCTION

by Arnold Kludas

One of the most fascinating chapters in the history of both technology and sociology is the evolution of the passenger liner. This book brings to life again the eventful and diverse 30 years between 1897 and 1927. The first vessels to deserve the title "luxury liner" had been the British-built sister ships *City of Paris* and *City of New York*, launched in 1888. It was the Cunarders *Campania* and *Lucania* of the early 1890s that elicited the massive German response with which this volume opens.

In 1897, when the four-funneled *Kaiser Wilhelm der Grosse* was launched, the Germans for the first time successfully challenged British supremacy on the North Atlantic. This North German Lloyd liner took the Blue Riband for speed away from Cunard. In all, five such German four-stackers were built up to 1907. But by that time these express steamers were no longer necessarily the biggest ships in the world. The use of steel now allowed shipbuilders to create vessels of practically unrestricted dimensions, and the White Star (second to Cunard in Britain) and Hamburg-America lines had given up the uneconomic competition for speed in favor of large ships emphasizing a high degree of luxury (their more moderate speed meant the absence of disturbing vibration, although that problem had already been nearly solved by the introduction of the steam turbine).

Maximum size, maximum speed and British supremacy all came together once more in the turbine-driven Cunard 30,000-tonners *Lusitania* and *Mauretania* (both 1907); the *Mauretania* retained the record for speed until 1929. The White Star Line countered in 1910 with the *Olympic*, the first ship of a new giant class of over 45,000 tons but, in accordance with the line's policy, with a maximum speed of only 21 knots.

Then, just as the ill-fated White Star *Titanic* met her tragic end on her maiden voyage in April 1912, another maritime superlative was ready for launching. The 52,000-ton *Imperator* (about five times the size of the *City of Paris* of 1888!) and her near-sister, the *Vaterland*, were the last word in shipbuilding and engineering prior to the First World War. They and their other sister, the *Bismarck*, remained the biggest ships in the world until 1935.

The First World War, which changed so many things, intervened, and altered ocean-liner plans and schemes. Many noted liners were sunk, the most famous of which was the *Lusitania*. Among the war victims were several great ships that had never seen any commercial service, such as the *Britannic* and *Statendam*, to name two of the largest. The end of the war meant for a time the end of international competition in building superliners. By 1926, however, the French were building a ship comparable to the big prewar liners and, more important, one that displayed new trends in interior styling and accommodation. This was, of course, the *Ile de France*. The present volume closes just before the appearance of this forerunner of the superliners of the thirties.

Of course, this work is not restricted to the crack liners of the North Atlantic, but also includes fascinating passenger ships on the other oceans and smaller—but still interesting—liners of all routes.

German Ship Museum, Bremerhaven
January 1984

THE EARLY FOUR-STACKERS

This is not simply a chapter of ships or even of maritime corporate rivalry, but also one of politics. In 1889, Germany's Kaiser Wilhelm II visited Britain's *Teutonic* of the White Star Line during a naval review at Spithead. The Emperor was deeply impressed. For the next 25 years or so, transatlantic passenger shipping would never be quite the same. Until then, the British had a monopoly of trans-ocean honors—the biggest, fastest and grandest passenger ships. The Kaiser was envious. When he returned to Germany, word spread quickly that Imperial maritime honor had to be established, reinforced, then reestablished again. After all, it was not simply a matter of outdoing the British but of clearly showing Europe and the rest of the world that the German Empire was reaching a new zenith of industrial and technological might.

It was eight years before the project could begin, before the first new German greyhound could be realized. The 14,300-ton *Kaiser Wilhelm der Grosse*, commissioned in September 1897, began the age of the great ocean liner. She also succeeded, quite happily, in her dual purpose. Not only was she the largest liner afloat, boasting the first four-funnel profile, but she grabbed the prized Blue Ribband for speed from the British. It was a serious blow to otherwise contented British Victorian pride. The Kaiser was delighted.

A corporate rivalry also developed. While the *Kaiser Wilhelm der Grosse* was owned by the North German Lloyd of Bremen, their archrival, the Hamburg-America Line of Hamburg, wanted their share, at least momentarily, of the honors. Thus in 1900 they commissioned the *Deutschland*, which in turn took the Blue Ribband. Nothing seemed quite as important as having the world's fastest ship. To the proud Germans, she was yet another marvel of their industrial stride.

The North German Lloyd responded with no fewer than three successively larger liners, all of them four-stackers, creating a quartet that would provide the best weekly express service on the North Atlantic. The three new vessels had the deep interest of the Kaiser and so, quite appropriately, bore royal names: *Kronprinz Wilhelm, Kaiser Wilhelm II* and *Kronprinzessin Cecilie*. It seemed that the Germans were undefeatable.

In 1905, the British Government was so worried about its strength of shipping on the Atlantic that it approached the Cunard Line to discuss at least two superships that, above all else, would be larger and faster than "those German monsters." Early projections to make the British liners as three-stackers had to be changed—the new ships would have four funnels, just like the German ships. In 1907, when this pair was commissioned as the *Lusitania* and *Mauretania*, the superlatives "largest" and "fastest" went back to Britain. (The distinction of "largest" remained until 1913, when the German *Imperator* first sailed from Hamburg, but the *Mauretania*'s speed was extraordinary and she held the Atlantic record until 1929.)

In response, the Germans lost their deep fascination with speed, at least for a time, and set out instead to concentrate on enormous size and superb luxury. National rivalries continued with the so-called "ships of state."

Of these early four-stackers, only the *Mauretania* survived intact after the First World War and consequently can be considered to have been the most successful. The *Kaiser Wilhelm der Grosse* and the *Lusitania* were both victims of the war, the German ship scuttled off West Africa, the Cunarder fatally pierced by a torpedo off Ireland. Three of the remaining Germans fell to the Americans during that war, ironically serving against the Kaiser who had been so instrumental in creating them. After the hostilities, no one knew quite what to do with them. There were proposals to reactivate them for liner service under the Stars and Stripes, but nothing ever came to pass. Each of them finished up in American scrapyards. The *Deutschland* seems to have been the only disappointment. Although she had captured the Blue Ribband, such prize-getting was done at the expense of operational performance. She was plagued, for most of her life, by noise and vibration from her powerful machinery. Hamburg-America, which placed passenger comfort above all else, could not have been more displeased. The *Deutschland* was eventually converted to a white-hulled cruise ship which did not require high speed. Finally, after the war, she was demoted to a twin-stack ship used for the transport of immigrants.

KAISER WILHELM DER GROSSE.

In the early 1890s, every record-breaking passenger ship on the North Atlantic was British-built. Imperial Germany, which had grown in strength both politically and technologically, was envious. Furthermore, the dominant German Atlantic passenger lines, the North German Lloyd of Bremen and the Hamburg-America Line of Hamburg, were in constant competition. Thus, with sufficient financial reserves and the ability to execute such a project in the home country, the North German Lloyd ordered a liner that would be not only the world's largest passenger ship but a speed-record-breaker as well.

In the presence of Kaiser Wilhelm II, the new ship was launched on May 3, 1897, as the *Kaiser Wilhelm der Grosse*, honoring the Kaiser's grandfather, Kaiser Wilhelm I. As the first four-stacker, the vessel might also be considered the first of the superliners. During her maiden crossing to New York that fall, thousands traveled to the dock and harbor areas of Bremerhaven, Southampton and New York for a glimpse of the German "wonder ship." Her record was just short of six days, surpassing the previous one held by Britain's *Lucania*, of the Cunard Line. As intended, a German liner had secured top honors and with them the attention of the entire world.

The workers at the tip of the bow of the *Kaiser Wilhelm der Grosse*, in dry dock for repairs *(opposite)*, give some indication of the size of the liner. The ship and, later, larger liners, required new and bigger pier and dry-dock facilities on both sides of the Atlantic. In 1899, the 722-foot Kaiser Dry Dock opened at Bremerhaven and ranked as the largest graving dock outside Britain. [Built by Vulkan Shipyards, Stettin, Germany, 1897. 14,349 gross tons; 655 feet long; 66 feet wide. Steam triple expansion engines geared to twin screw. Service speed 22 knots. 1,970 passengers (558 first class, 338 second class, 1,074 steerage).]

The *Kaiser Wilhelm der Grosse*. Passenger ships such as the *Kaiser Wilhelm der Grosse* relied on coal as a source of fuel. The loading process for each voyage was often cumbersome, dirty and time-consuming. In the view above, the liner is being coaled at Bremerhaven in preparation for her next crossing. Another North German Lloyd liner, the *Bremen* of 1900, is docked at the right.

As on the four other German four-stackers, the funnels on the *Kaiser Wilhelm der Grosse* were grouped two and two, a unique design concept that always made such German liners clearly recognizable. The scheme had more practical reasons: the pairing eliminated the need for funnel shafts in the first-class restaurant and also provided better exhausts for the below-deck boilers. Because of the publicity that surrounded the ship's size and speed, the number of stacks on the *Kaiser Wilhelm der Grosse* was quickly thought by the traveling public to be a clear indication of both great size (and therefore great safety) as well as great speed. Quite simply, the theory of the day was "the more stacks, the better the ship." The highly sought revenue-producing immigrant trade—those thousands who were seeking one-way passages to America—used this system in selecting the ship for their "voyage of a lifetime." There were occasions when steamer companies misrepresented their ships as having more stacks than they had in reality, causing riots on sailing day. Some passengers would steadfastly refuse to sail until rebooked on a liner with at least three—but preferably four—funnels.

Gilded Age elegance on board the *Kaiser Wilhelm der Grosse*. The first-class dining room *(opposite, top)* could seat all 558 first-class passengers at a single sitting. The room itself could be converted into larger spaces by opening a series of doors. The tufted-leather sofas of a sitting room *(opposite, bottom)* create a charming atmosphere in first class aboard the German speed queen.

DEUTSCHLAND (1900; *above*).

North German Lloyd's German archrival was the Hamburg-America Line. In fact, it was a rivalry between two great seaports: the Lloyd at Bremen and Hapag (an abbreviation for Hamburg-America) at Hamburg.

Hapag, deeply impressed and envious of the Lloyd's *Kaiser Wilhelm der Grosse*, proceeded to build a large record-breaker of its own. This ship, commissioned in the summer of 1900 as the *Deutschland*, immediately took the coveted Blue Ribband, an honor she held for the next six years. But she was to be the only speed queen in the Hamburg-America fleet. While the directorate of the North German Lloyd and several other transatlantic companies remained obsessed with record crossings, the Hamburg-America management shifted its future emphasis in liner building to two other elements: great luxury and size. To some extent, the *Deutschland* prompted this decision because she had proved to be operationally unsatisfactory. She was plagued with vibrations from her high-speed engines as well as with excessive rattling and noise that disturbed her passengers. In 1910–11 she was rebuilt completely with far less powerful engines. Thereafter she was used as a cruise ship.

The *Deutschland's* first-class café *(left)* proved to be a popular gathering spot. The Hamburg-America Line always emphasized passenger comfort, even in third class and steerage. Company officials were often seen on board passenger ships, pad and pencil in hand, making notes on possible improvements.

As the largest ship of her time, the *Deutschland* towered above the tenements, factories and pier sheds of Hoboken, where she docked at the Second Street Pier *(opposite, top)*. The piers in this photo lasted only a short time. By 1910, a new set of 1,000-footers was completed, designed and built especially for Hamburg-America's new breed of giant Atlantic liners, the ships of 900 feet and over—the *Imperator*, *Vaterland* and *Bismarck*. [Built by Vulkan Shipyards, Stettin, Germany, 1900. 16,502 gross tons; 684 feet long; 67 feet wide. Quadruple expansion engines geared to twin screw. Service speed 22 knots. 2,050 passengers (450 first class, 300 second class, 300 third class, 1,000 steerage).]

VICTORIA LUISE (above).

Despite her success in securing the Blue Ribband for the Hamburg-America Line for six years, the *Deutschland* was an unsatisfactory liner, as already explained. When, in 1905–06, the company decided to stress size and luxury, the fate of the troubled *Deutschland* was set. However, she survived another four years on the North Atlantic run to New York, before her re-engining and conversion to a cruise ship.

The former *Deutschland* reappeared at the end of 1911 as the *Victoria Luise*, repainted in a white hull and with the reputation as the finest cruising liner afloat. Considering her 16,700 tons and 684-foot length, she offered very luxurious all-first-class accommodations for a mere 487 guests. Her leisurely travels now took her to the West Indies, the Mediterranean and Scandinavia and on occasion she acted as "host ship" for Imperial German aristocracy for naval reviews and official regattas.

The *Victoria Luise* remained idle in Germany during the First World War, mainly because of her operational problems. In 1919, after the surrender, she was the only large national steamer not to be handed over to the victorious Allies, again because of her engine difficulties. She was rebuilt in 1921 as the immigrant ship *Hansa* and survived until 1925, when she was scrapped at Hamburg.

KRONPRINZ WILHELM *(opposite, top).*

In response to the blazing success of the *Kaiser Wilhelm der Grosse* and then of the *Deutschland* of the rival Hamburg-America Line, the North German Lloyd commissioned their second four-stacker in September 1901. Named for the German crown prince, this new liner was christened as the *Kronprinz Wilhelm*. As an express liner for the run between Bremerhaven and New York, this ship was intended to recapture the famed Blue Ribband from the *Deutschland*. She never quite succeeded. Her machinery could not muster the additional power to surpass the *Deutschland's* record. However, in all other ways, she was pleasing to her owners. She was one of the largest and most luxurious liners afloat, and was an important part of the North German express team of a quartet of four-stackers: the *Kaiser Wilhelm der Grosse* of 1897, the *Kronprinz Wilhelm* of 1901, the *Kaiser Wilhelm II* of 1903 and finally the *Kronprinzessin Cecilie* of 1906.

Accommodations on board the *Kronprinz Wilhelm* were divided into three classes: first, second and the very lucrative steerage. First class contained the most space and included salons of carved wood and magnificent art, suites and staterooms with marble bathrooms and special sitting rooms. A deluxe suite aboard the *Kronprinz Wilhelm* in 1901 could cost as much as $2,000 for a week's crossing. Second class was a modified version of first class, but with far less opulence and space. The steerage quarters, the most profitable to the company, were given the smallest amount of space and certainly the least amount of comfort. For those in steerage, the voyage to America could cost as little as $10.

Crewmen attend to necessary maintenance aboard the *Kronprinz Wilhelm (opposite)*, then one of the world's largest liners, at the North German Lloyd piers in Hoboken. [Built by Vulkan Shipyards, Stettin, Germany, 1901. 14,908 gross tons; 664 feet long; 66 feet wide. Steam quadruple expansion engines geared to twin screw. Service speed 22 knots. 1,761 passengers (367 first class, 340 second class, 1,054 steerage).]

KAISER WILHELM II *(above, right).*

The third of the North German Lloyd four-stackers was the *Kaiser Wilhelm II*, completed in the spring of 1903. She was longer and considerably larger than the previous express liners. She was also intended to break the speed record, but did not succeed until June 1906, when she took the Blue Ribband from Hamburg-America's *Deutschland*. She maintained the honored position as world's fastest ship (passenger liner or otherwise) until the following year, when Britain recaptured the glory with the Cunard sisters *Lusitania* and *Mauretania*.

Like all of the other German four-stackers, the *Kaiser Wilhelm II's* success was determined to a great extent by early public-relations men. Her maiden arrival in New York harbor consisted of such a great press effort, promoting her size, speed and magnificent interiors, that some 40,000 visitors came on board for inspection during the initial call. This was a figure larger than the entire population of the city of Hoboken, where the liner was berthed.

Celebrity passengers often crossed on the German greyhounds *(right)*. Metropolitan Opera stars Johanna Gadski (seated, left) and Enrico Caruso (seated, with camera) are seen with family and friends aboard the *Kaiser Wilhelm II* in September 1903. [Built by Vulkan Shipyards, Stettin, Germany, 1903. 19,361 gross tons; 707 feet long; 72 feet wide. Steam quadruple expansion engines geared to twin screw. Service speed 23 knots. 1,888 passengers (775 first class, 343 second class, 770 steerage).]

KRONPRINZESSIN CECILIE (opposite).

The last four-stacker to fly the German flag was North German Lloyd's *Kronprinzessin Cecilie*. The completion of the company's four-liner express service, the best of its kind in the world, provided a weekly sailing from either New York or Bremerhaven. It was a popular, exact service that served thousands of passengers.

The *Kronprinzessin Cecilie* was not particularly distinctive (she was not the world's largest or fastest) but she was one of the finest, most luxurious liners of her day. Her first-class accommodations were so luxurious that the suites included small, separate private dining rooms for the more reclusive travelers—the American millionaires who frequently used the ship. The first-class restaurant included a fish tank to provide fresh dinnertime selections.

Of course, like her earlier German predecessors and other contemporaries, the *Kronprinzessin Cecilie* also carried steerage passengers. The facilities were in marked contrast to the upper-deck

luxuries of first class. By 1910, the differences were best exemplified in the cost of a week's passage to America: $2,500 for a top suite in first class as compared to $25 in steerage.

The four great mustard-colored stacks of the *Kronprinzessin Cecilie (below, left)* were photographed while the liner was at dock at the Third Street Pier in Hoboken. The early theory that more stacks meant greater safety, security and size persisted on the North Atlantic liner run for many years. Consequently, the three- and four-funnel liners were almost always the most popular ships, especially with the immigrant trade.

The first-class salon *(below, right)* reflects the quality of the craftsmanship then available. [Built by Vulcan Shipyards, Stettin, Germany, 1906. 19,360 gross tons; 707 feet long; 72 feet wide. Steam quadruple expansion engines geared to twin screw. Service speed 23 knots. 1,970 passengers (558 first class, 338 second class, 1,074 steerage).]

LUSITANIA *(above)* **and MAURETANIA** *(opposite)*.

The British government was unhappy at the turn of the century because of the dominance of the German four-stackers on the prestigious North Atlantic run. The situation was further aggravated when the nation's second-largest liner firm, the White Star Company, was sold to the J. P. Morgan interests in America. Even if the White Star ships would continue to fly the British ensign, they were still American-owned. To salvage national prestige, the government turned to the Cunard Line, then the biggest operation on the Atlantic, and offered a liberal construction loan as well as an operating mail subsidy for not one, but two large express liners. They became the biggest and fastest ships afloat. They were also to represent British technology and supposed supremacy in marine engineering and design. The selection of machinery for the new super-Cunarders, following a very successful experiment with the then very new steam-turbine system of propulsion aboard the Cunarder *Carmania* in 1905, was considered quite startling. It was, in fact, to begin the age of the more efficient and powerful steam-turbine-powered liner.

The new twin liners followed the Cunard naming practice of using Roman geographic names. The first of the pair, the *Lusitania*, was named for Roman Portugal, while the *Mauretania* took hers from Roman Morocco. Both ships were far bigger than the earlier standard established by the German four-stackers, each being well over 10,000 tons larger. They were given nicely balanced profiles of twin masts and four evenly spaced funnels, each done in Cunard's orange-red and black. Their statistics were mind-boggling at the time. For example, there were 25 boilers and 192 furnaces aboard each ship, with a storage capacity for 6,000 tons of coal, which produced a service speed of 24–25 knots or the consumption of 1,000 tons of coal per day.

The *Lusitania*, shown here leaving New York with the unfinished Singer Tower rising in the background, was commissioned in September 1907; the *Mauretania* in November. [*Lusitania*: Built by John Brown & Company Limited, Clydebank, Scotland, 1907. 31,550 gross tons; 787 feet long; 87 feet wide. Steam turbines geared to quadruple screw. Service speed 25 knots. 2,165 passengers (563 first class, 464 second class, 1,138 third class).]

If the *Lusitania* was later the victim of a tragic sinking off Ireland in 1915, the *Mauretania* was one of the most successful liners ever built. After the *Lusitania* captured the Blue Ribband with the first average speed greater than 25 knots in 1907, her maiden year, Britain was to retain the speed honors for well over two decades. Soon after the *Lusitania*'s triumph, the *Mauretania* made an even faster run, above 26 knots, and eventually established herself as the faster of the pair and the holder of the Blue Ribband. For this distinction (lasting until 1929), more travelers often preferred the *Mauretania*. The British Government and Cunard were rightly proud of their speedy sister ships and more specifically of the *Mauretania* herself. The Germans were furious. [*Mauretania*: Built by Swan, Hunter & Wigham Richardson Limited, Newcastle, England, 1907. 31,938 gross tons; 790 feet long; 88 feet wide. Steam turbines geared to quadruple screw. Service speed 25 knots. 2,335 passengers (560 first class, 475 second class, 1,300 third class).]

A group of passengers *(overleaf)* was photographed along the upper decks of the giant *Lusitania* in 1908, when the liner berthed at the foot of West 14th Street in Manhattan.

The *Lusitania* and *Mauretania*. The interiors represented the glories of British and European design. The forests of England and France were scoured for the most perfect woods, some of which were exquisitely carved in great detail. The decor themes ranged from French Renaissance to English Country and included lavish lounges, smoking rooms (such as the one aboard the *Lusitania, opposite*), libraries, salons, private parlors and even an exceptional palm court.

All of the ships' bathroom fixtures in first class were silver-plated while those in second and third class were done in then-new white metals. Magnificent rails and bronze work surrounded this elevator cage aboard the *Lusitania (above)* while the *Mauretania* was dubiously distinctive in having the first hydraulically operated barber's chair.

The *Lusitania* and *Mauretania*. The wood paneling in first class aboard the *Mauretania* was carved to perfection by 300 craftsmen brought from Palestine to the shipyards in England. During the day, the liner's smoking room, always kept in glistening perfection, was flooded with sunlight from a skylight.

SUITES, SALONS AND STEERAGE

First and foremost, the owners of passenger ships were business people. Their ships were built in response to trading conditions, to repay their costs and then to earn profits for their owners. For the most part, the prestigious titles of "world's largest" and "world's fastest" were of interest only to the major firms, those four or five operators who maintained sizable, often government-inspired and financed fleets. Assuredly, the so-called largest and fastest liners were never harmed by such distinctions. There was always a constant flow of travelers who sought the opportunity to send postcard messages from "the largest" (or "fastest") "ship afloat."

But for the numerous other ships and their owners, operations were prompted by the growth of the more ordinary travelers in first and second class, and by the massive exodus of immigrants to the shores of North America. Lacking the distinctive superlatives of, say, some of the British and German firms were shipowners such as the Red Star Line of Belgium, the Scandinavian-American Line of Denmark and the Holland-America Line. In the pages of this chapter are some of those less-famous ships: the *Lapland*, the *Frederik VIII* and the first *Nieuw Amsterdam*. The ships have been grouped by flag, owner or trade. As

always, the Atlantic passenger liners are featured most prominently.

First and second class offered quarters that featured varying degrees of comfort. There were staterooms priced according to size, convenience and shipboard location—all combined with a series of public rooms (the smoking rooms, lounges, salons and dining rooms) that made for a pleasant one- or two-week crossing. But for most of the passenger firms, the deepest interest was in the third-class and steerage spaces. This interest was not based on providing much comfort, but on the great profits secured from those "masses" seeking passage to the New World. Quite simply, the steamer companies made the most money on those passengers who paid the lowest fares ($25 or less), had the fewest accommodations and were given the least provision and service. The steamship firms made handsome profits. Every passenger ship, from the large, luxurious likes of the *Mauretania* and even the *Titanic* to a near-endless list of smaller vessels, was fitted to carry steerage passengers. Over 1.2 million immigrants arrived in New York harbor in 1907, for example. Every one of them arrived by ship.

CAMPANIA *(opposite, top).*
Cunard's fleet of Atlantic liners was, at the turn of the century, rapidly modernizing and expanding. When she was completed in 1893, the *Campania* (seen here) and her sister *Lucania* were the largest passenger ships afloat, at 12,900 tons each. They were also the fastest, with record speeds of over 21 knots. Fourteen years later, in 1907, Cunard was highlighted by the sisters *Lusitania* and *Mauretania*, at some 31,000 tons each and with record speeds of over 25 knots. Early notable ships like the *Campania* were being quickly relegated to secondary positions by the rapid and extreme advances in industrial and technological development. [Built by the Fairfield Shipbuilding & Engineering Company, Glasgow, Scotland, 1893. 12,950 gross tons; 622 feet long; 65 feet wide. Steam triple expansion engines geared to twin screw. Service speed 21 knots. 2,000 passengers (600 first class, 400 second class, 1,000 steerage).]

IVERNIA *(opposite, bottom).*
As did most North Atlantic firms, Cunard maintained a separate fleet of intermediate, auxiliary passenger ships that catered to the vast immigrant trade. These ships, designed for more functional purposes, generally lacked the glamor and reputation of the larger liners. The *Ivernia* was such a ship, working on Cunard's service from Liverpool to Boston and later on the immigrant run from Trieste to New York. She did have one distinction: the largest single funnel ever fitted to a ship, measuring 60 feet from the top deck. [Built by Swan, Hunter & Wigham Richardson Limited, Newcastle, England, 1900. 13,799 gross tons; 600 feet long; 64 feet wide. Steam quadruple expansion engines geared to twin screw. Service speed 15 knots. 1,964 passengers (164 first class, 200 second class, 1,600 steerage).]

CARMANIA *(above)* **and CARONIA.**
The Cunard sister ships *Caronia* and *Carmania* were two of the most important passenger ships of the early years of the twentieth century. However, they were known more for their machinery than for their size or luxury. Cunard, as the largest firm on the transatlantic passenger run, was intrigued by the new concept of steam-turbine drive. The earlier system of steam-reciprocating engines was not as efficient and was often dirty. Company directors selected the new sisters for experimentation. The *Caronia* was fitted with the older-style machinery; the *Carmania*, seen here, with the new turbines. The latter proved to be far superior, making for a faster and cleaner operation. In quick time, the designers of the much larger *Lusitania* and *Mauretania*, also of Cunard, selected the new steam turbines. The decision again moved Britain to the forefront of marine design and engineering. Thereafter, most major Atlantic liners were built with steam-turbine propulsion. [*Carmania*: Built by John Brown & Company Limited, Clydebank, Scotland, 1905. 19,524 gross tons; 675 feet long; 72 feet wide. Steam turbines geared to triple screw. Service speed 18 knots. 2,650 passengers (300 first class, 350 second class, 900 third class, 1,100 steerage).]

The *Carmania* and *Caronia*. The *Caronia (above)* and the *Carmania* were known, because of their good looks, as the "pretty sisters." They worked Cunard's mainline Atlantic service between Liverpool and New York. In this scene the *Caronia* prepares for a Saturday morning sailing from her Lower Manhattan pier. The ice-filled waters of the Hudson River can be seen on the right. [*Caronia*: Built by John Brown & Company Limited, Clydebank, Scotland, 1905. 19,524 gross tons; 678 feet long; 72 feet wide. Steam quadruple expansion engines geared to twin screw. Service speed 18 knots. 2,650 passengers (300 first class, 350 second class, 900 third class, 1,100 steerage).]

The *Caronia*'s smoking room *(opposite, top)* had a distinctly "clubby" feeling.

Skylights and domed ceilings were frequent decorative elements in the first-class public rooms of transatlantic liners. The glassed ceiling allowed for a bright, cheerful use of this lounge aboard the *Caronia (opposite, bottom)* during daylight hours. At night, the room had a very soft, almost semidark appearance with illumination provided by wall and ceiling lamps with exposed bulbs.

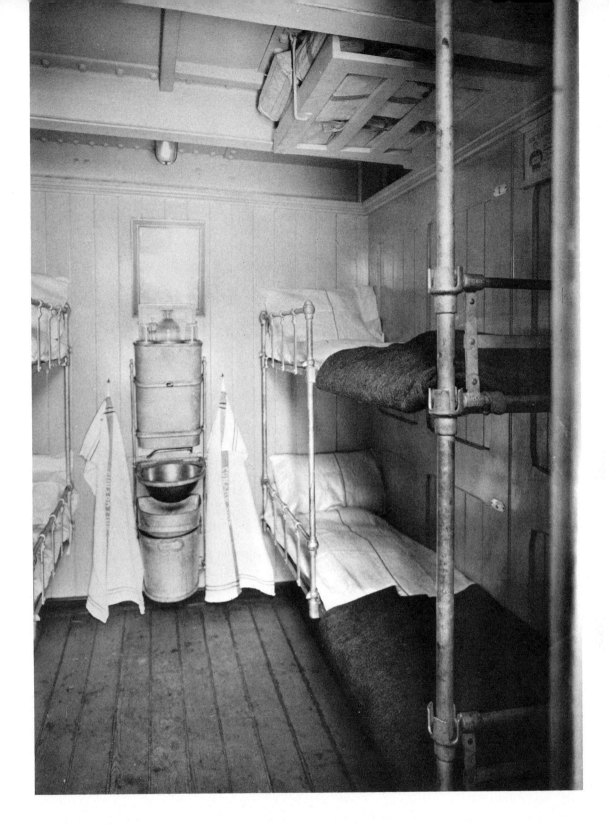

The *Carmania* and *Caronia*. First-class staterooms aboard the *Caronia (opposite, top)* were often interconnecting for family travel. Private bathroom facilities were a rarity, except in the most expensive suites. Public facilities were usually available on the same deck, in an inside position along the corridor. Passengers made reservations for a bath with their cabin steward, who in turn notified the bath steward. Daily bathing, even in first class, was not a common practice aboard the liners in the early years of this century. Furthermore, warm water for shaving and washing was available only through the cabin steward, who delivered it at appointed times. Cabin faucets, if available, offered only cold water. An electric floor heater stands in the cabin shown here. Except in the main lounges, heating was not necessarily provided on turn-of-the-century steamers.

This second-class lounge aboard the *Caronia (opposite, bottom)* although pleasant and seemingly comfortable, lacked the more ornate styling found in first class.

In contrast to the refinements of first and second class were the accommodations in third class or steerage *(above)*. In 1910, passengers might pay $25 for a berth in such a room (this one is on the *Caronia*) for the eight-to-ten-day crossing to America. Public washing and toilet facilities in steerage were often too few in numbers to cater adequately to the number of passengers. Sinks on the *Caronia*, for example, were part of the limited accommodations for the 900 passengers in third class and the 1,100 in steerage.

OCEANIC.

The White Star Line was in almost constant competition with Cunard. Each year, these companies would introduce yet-larger, faster and more luxurious passenger ships. Publicists worked hard in explaining the greater refinements of first class and also the supposedly improved, more spacious quarters in steerage. But, as in the past, the most popular ships were those which were larger (or at least appeared so) and which looked safe and dependable.

When completed in 1899, White Star's *Oceanic* was the biggest ship afloat. She was the first ship to exceed 700 feet in length.

Such large liners were feared by small-craft operators, in this age before radar and other ship-spotting devices. Collision, especially in fog, was a horrifying possibility and all too often a reality. In September 1901, the *Oceanic* rammed a small coastal freighter off the British coast. Seven were lost. The year before, the Cunarder *Campania* sliced in half a bark in the Irish Sea. Eleven died. In 1908, the American liner *St. Paul* collided with the British cruiser *Gladiator*. The small warship sank, taking 27 lives. [Built by Harland & Wolff Limited, Belfast, Northern Ireland, 1899. 17,272 gross tons; 704 feet long; 63 feet wide. Steam triple expansion engines geared to twin screw. Service speed 19 knots. 1,710 passengers (410 first class, 300 second class, 1,000 steerage).]

CELTIC *(opposite, top).*

In 1900, when White Star decided upon two more of the larger Atlantic liners, the cherished factors of size and dependability were included in the planning. A year later, when the *Celtic* was commissioned, she was the largest liner afloat, the first to exceed 20,000 tons. Furthermore, instead of having three or four funnels, the design pattern was reversed somewhat: four masts and two rather thin stacks. The number of masts was intended to be a reminder of the great sailing ships of the previous century. White Star felt that potential passengers wanted a conservative, sound-looking vessel—not one that simply opted for a more modern approach. The theory worked. The *Celtic* and her sister, the *Cedric*, delivered in 1903, were among the most successful liners on the North Atlantic. [Built by Harland & Wolff Limited, Belfast, Northern Ireland, 1901. 20,904 gross tons; 700 feet long; 75 feet wide. Steam quadruple expansion engines geared to twin screw. Service speed 16 knots. 2,857 passengers (347 first class, 160 second class, 2,350 steerage).]

BALTIC *(opposite, bottom).*

So popular were the *Celtic* and *Cedric* that the White Star Line ordered two similar ships, slightly larger still. Named the *Baltic* and the *Adriatic*, they completed a quartet known as "The Big Four"—the largest liners in the world, for a few years at least. The pairing also created a weekly service between Liverpool and New York, with a stop in Ireland, primarily for immigrants.

White Star directors were so pleased with these four ships that attention turned to far larger liners, three ships (they would be-

come the *Olympic, Titanic* and *Britannic*) that could maintain a weekly service with yet even higher standards of luxury. [Built by Harland & Wolff Limited, Belfast, Northern Ireland, 1904. 23,884 gross tons; 726 feet long; 75 feet wide. Steam quadruple expansion engines geared to twin screw. Service speed 16 knots. 2,875 passengers (425 first class, 450 second class, 2,000 steerage).]

REPUBLIC *(above).*

White Star, like Cunard and many other liner companies, maintained a secondary fleet of auxiliary passenger ships that catered mostly to the booming immigrant trade to North America. However, one of these ships, White Star's *Republic*, achieved a historic milestone in an otherwise short, unnoticed career. On January 23, 1909, the *Republic* collided with the Italian steamer *Florida* just off the Nantucket Lightship. With over 2,000 people aboard, the *Republic* was badly damaged and in need of assistance. She sent the first S.O.S. radio distress message in the history of sea travel. As a result, all but four of her passengers and crew were saved by nearby rescue ships. The new distress system was soon used by vessels throughout the world. The damage to the *Republic* proved fatal. Some small American freighters attempted to tow her to safety, but the empty ship sank on the morning of January 24. [Built by Harland & Wolff Limited, Belfast, Northern Ireland, 1903. 15,378 gross tons; 585 feet long; 67 feet wide. Steam quadruple expansion engines geared to twin screw. Service speed 16 knots. Approximately 200 first-class passengers, over 2,000 steerage).]

EMPRESS OF IRELAND (above).

The Canadian Pacific system created the largest transportation network on earth. Passenger ships worked the North Atlantic, connecting Britain with Eastern Canada. A rail link was developed to reach British Columbia, terminating at the Pacific port of Vancouver. From there, a second set of steamers traded to the Orient. Passengers seeking an alternative route to, say, Hong Kong or Japan could avoid the long, hot and often uncomfortable passage via Suez. Soon, as a result of its great success, Canadian Pacific acquired many of its competitors (Cunard being one exception) on the Atlantic.

The *Empress* liners were the hallmarks of the Canadian Pacific shipping system on both oceans. Two of the largest passenger ships on the North Atlantic were the 14,200-ton sisters *Empress of Britain* and *Empress of Ireland*, both commissioned in 1906, for the run between Liverpool and Quebec City. Unfortunately, the memory of the *Empress of Ireland* is scarred with tragedy. On May 29, 1914, while in the St. Lawrence River near Father Point, she was rammed in a thick fog by the poorly navigated Norwegian steamer *Storstad*. The *Empress* sank almost immediately, claiming some 1,024 lives. The *Titanic* had sunk two years earlier with the loss of 1,503 people, and these two tragedies represented the worst sea disasters to date. [Built by the Fairfield Shipbuilding & Engineering Company, Glasgow, Scotland, 1906. 14,191 gross tons; 570 feet long; 65 feet wide. Steam quadruple expansion engines geared to twin screw. Service speed 18 knots. 1,580 passengers (310 first class, 500 second class, 500 third class, 270 steerage).]

KÖNIG ALBERT (opposite).

The Hamburg-America Line and North German Lloyd were among the very few steamer companies actually to own their pier facilities in New York harbor. Located in Hoboken, just across from West 10th Street in Manhattan, the four finger piers stretched into the Hudson for three city blocks. Able to handle some of the world's largest liners, these docks were built on piles of from 50 to 90 feet that were driven through the soft river mud at six-foot intervals.

The German pier complex in Hoboken included workshops and storerooms, an engine plant with a boiler house, a coal shed, a smithy, a storeroom for cordage and other loading and discharging tackle, a storeroom for lamps and other lighting articles, a cooper's shop, a storeroom for coaling gear, a painter's shop, a sailmakers' shop, a large baggage room, fifteen offices representing different steamship departments, a separate railway system and a superintendent's apartment that included a portable rooftop swimming pool for summer afternoons.

In this scene, North German Lloyd's intermediate steamer *König Albert* rests at the Hoboken piers. [Built by Vulkan Shipyards, Stettin, Germany, 1899. 10,484 gross tons; 521 feet long; 60 feet wide. Steam quadruple expansion engines geared to twin screw. Service speed 15.5 knots. 2,175 passengers (257 first class, 119 second class, 1,799 steerage).]

Byron
N.Y.
24350

HAMBURG *(opposite)*.
Distinguished passengers often passed through the Hoboken terminal. In these scenes shown, former President Teddy Roosevelt is departing for Africa aboard the *Hamburg* of the Hamburg-America Line. [Built by Vulkan Shipyards, Stettin, Germany, 1900. 10,532 gross tons; 521 feet long; 60 feet wide. Quadruple expansion engines geared to twin screw. Service speed 15.3 knots. 2,170 passengers (290 first class, 100 second class, 80 third class, 1,700 steerage).]

THE HOBOKEN FIRE *(above)*.
The original German liner piers in Hoboken were destroyed in a giant fire that erupted on an otherwise quiet Saturday afternoon, June 30, 1900. The blaze, caused by spontaneous combustion, broke out in a tall stack of bailed cargo on Pier 3. Simultaneously, this blocked the escape of hundreds of passengers, crew and visitors who were on board four liners. Three of the liners were engulfed quickly in flames. The *Saale* was lost completely and the *Main* and *Bremen* run aground. 215 lives were lost by fire or by drowning in the murky waters of the Hudson. Some were unable to escape from their burning ships because of the small size of the portholes. Following this tragedy, the size of all portholes was increased to suit at least a full-grown man. The fire burned for three days and caused $10 million in damages. A new series of steel piers was completed by 1905, just in time for a new breed of larger German liners.

AMERIKA (opposite, top).

When the Hamburg-America Line's *Amerika* was first commissioned in October 1905, she ranked as the largest and one of the most luxurious and noteworthy liners afloat. Intensive American press efforts surrounded most of the large German liners. The public was flooded with information on the grandeurs of their accommodations, the power of their machinery and even such lesser details as the number of teacups used on board or the length of the electric wiring if stretched end to end. Illustrated literature detailed her splendors—from the wood panels in the first-class smoking room to the lush greenery in the winter garden. Special note was made of the liner's elevator, the first ever installed in a passenger ship. As a result of this publicity, many German liners were better known in America than in Germany itself. [Built by Harland & Wolff Limited, Belfast, Northern Ireland, 1905. 22,225 gross tons; 700 feet long; 74 feet wide. Steam quadruple expansion engines geared to twin screw. Service speed 17.5 knots. 2,662 passengers (420 first class, 254 second class, 223 third class, 1,765 steerage).]

KAISERIN AUGUSTE VICTORIA
(opposite, bottom; above).

Within a year, a near-sister to the *Amerika* was commissioned. Christened by the Empress of Germany, she was named *Kaiserin Auguste Victoria* and she became, for a brief time, the world's largest liner. But again, Hamburg-America was more concerned with extreme comfort and luxury. Therefore, one of the novelties in the ship's first-class accommodations was a special grill room, managed by the famed Ritz Carlton Company. Gold-trimmed menu cards featured such items as whole roast oxen and grilled antelope. But even for those first-class travelers, there was an additional admittance fee. Ironically, this surcharge could cost as much as a passage ticket in steerage.

Along with pleasures of their upper-deck passenger accommodations, the Germans stressed the technological side of the passenger ship. There were near-poetic descriptions of "great works of steel and power that moved across the sea." Consequently, publicity material often included at least one view of the liner's mechanical side. The scene above shows one of the *Kaiserin Auguste Victoria*'s twin propeller shafts. Prospective passengers and other enthusiasts were conscientiously told that such equipment helped to drive a near-25,000-ton liner at a speed of over 17 knots or nearly 20 miles per hour. In the age long before speedy aircraft, the ocean liner was one of the most marvelous objects of industrial and national progress. [Built by Vulkan Shipyards, Stettin, Germany, 1906. 24,581 gross tons; 705 feet long; 77 feet wide. Steam quadruple expansion engines geared to twin screw. Service speed 17.5 knots. 2,996 passengers (652 first class, 286 second class, 216 third class, 1,842 steerage).]

The *Kaiserin Auguste Victoria*. Hamburg-America was among the first of the Atlantic liner companies to use publicity photographs for their advertising. A model posed as a passenger *(above)* appears to be preparing for a journey in one of the Imperial Suites aboard the *Kaiserin Auguste Victoria*.

The same model is joined by several other "hired" passengers, all simulating a casual afternoon along the promenade deck *(opposite, top)*. The ship's orchestra is posed, suggesting the customary offering of a midday concert on deck. In reality, such photo sessions were usually done aboard empty and quiet liners that were, in fact, secured to their Hoboken pier in the calm waters of New York harbor.

A Hamburg-America brochure of 1909 used a photo suggesting that most famous of shipboard deck games: shuffleboard *(opposite, bottom)*. More than most other Atlantic firms, the Germans emphasized the healthy pursuit of top-deck pastimes. To many, the sea voyage had enormous salutary qualities.

PRESIDENT LINCOLN.

The Germans had passenger ships that earned their keep in several ways. Aboard the *President Lincoln*, there were token first- and second-class accommodations but almost mind-boggling capacities in third class and steerage for that endless stream of immigrants seeking westward passage. For slack sailings and the homebound runs to Germany, such ships had six large cargo holds. The *President Lincoln* was a clever blend of passenger and cargo operations.

The only six-masted passenger ships ever built, the *President Lincoln (opposite, top)* and her sister, the *President Grant*, reflected an attempt by the Germans to lure more immigrants aboard their ships. By using American names (others included *Cleveland, Cincinnati* and even *Amerika* and *George Washington*), it was reasoned that more America-bound immigrants would be attracted. To some extent, this plan succeeded. Many immigrants selected these ships, assuming that their entry process and naturalization would be better achieved. [Built by Harland & Wolff Limited, Belfast, Northern Ireland, 1907. 18,168 gross tons; 616 feet long; 68 feet wide. Steam quadruple expansion engines geared to twin screw. Service speed 14.5 knots. 3,828 passengers (324 first class, 152 second class, 1,004 third class, 2,348 steerage).]

Starched napkins in the first-class dining room *(opposite, bottom)* suggest a regatta of sailboats.

In the kitchens aboard *(above)* meals had to be prepared at least twice a day for the 3,828 passengers and 344 crew members.

The difference between third class and steerage aboard the ship was in accommodation. Third class *(right)* had cabins, no matter how stark and uninviting. Steerage passengers were berthed in vast open, dormitory-like spaces on iron-tube bunks.

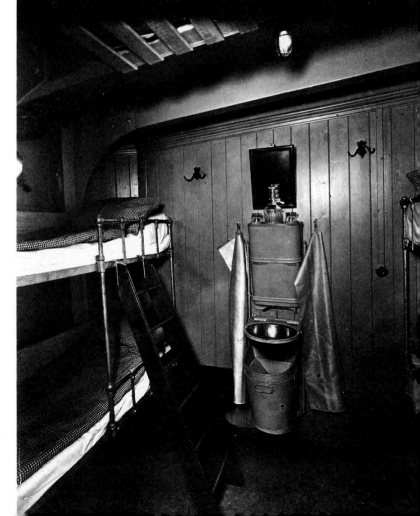

PATRICIA.

Immigrants rest on the deck of Hamburg-America's *Patricia (opposite, top)*. Most of the larger steamship companies had internment "villages" for the third-class and steerage immigrants at their European terminal ports. Prior to boarding the liners for the "voyage of a lifetime" to America, they would arrive by train from various parts of Europe. They would wait at these "villages" (some companies preferred to call them "hotels"), often being instructed on the crossing and the ship itself, and on the American entry process. [Built by Vulkan Shipyards, Stettin, Germany, 1899. 13,023 gross tons; 585 feet long; 62 feet wide. Steam quadruple expansion engines geared to twin screw. Service speed 13 knots. 2,489 passengers (162 first class, 184 second class, 2,143 steerage).]

Between 1900 and 1915, 12.5 million immigrants crossed the Atlantic to the New World (1.2 million in 1907 alone). Nearly 90 percent of them made the journey in third class or steerage. The peak years seem to have been between 1903 and 1907, and 1910 to 1915. The total list is staggering: 3 million from Italy; 3 million from the Balkan countries; 2.5 million from Russia and the Baltic countries; nearly 1 million from Britain; another 1 million from Scandinavia; 500,000 from Ireland; 500,000 from Germany; and more than 1 million from other European nations.

At European ports, immigrants were often put aboard passenger steamers by heavily loaded tenders *(opposite, bottom)*—smaller vessels that were often owned by the liner firms themselves. In the view above, immigrants are boarding Hamburg-America's *Patricia* but from a Holland-America Line tender (note that company's funnel design at the right).

Although most immigrants endured crowded and cramped quarters aboard Atlantic liners, the passage was not always unbearable. A sample steerage menu from a Holland-America liner in 1905 consisted of such main meals as: Monday—sauerkraut with smoked bacon and potatoes; Tuesday—pea soup, salted bacon and potatoes; Wednesday—brown bean soup, salted meat, potatoes and groats; Thursday—vegetable soup, beef with potatoes and rice; Friday—pea soup, salted bacon and potatoes; Saturday—white bean soup, salted meat and potatoes; and Sunday—vegetable soup, beef with potatoes and rice.

At New York, third-class and steerage passengers were unloaded from steamers anchored in the lower reaches of the harbor. Those immigrant passengers were taken by tenders, ferries and barges to Ellis Island, the Government inspection station situated in the shadow of the Statue of Liberty. Only the first- and second-class passengers were permitted to remain and proceed to the Manhattan docks.

More than a third of the people living in the United States today arrived via Ellis Island or had relatives who did. To the immigrants, the inspection process was terrifying, even more so than the crossing itself. Ellis Island doctors were known as the "six-second specialists," checking immigrants who showed possible symptoms of disease—heavy breathing, limping, coughing and even thinning hair. If a doctor made a chalk mark on an immigrant's coat (such as E for eye, L for limp and so forth), it indicated further medical inspection. For the immigrants, it was yet more fear.

In the second phase of the inspection, immigration officials checked information that had already been collected by the steamship firms. In this process, through misunderstandings and the diverse mixture of foreign languages, names were often changed. For example, Bugajsky became Baglinsky. Fishcov became Fishman. One of the more noted cases was the three brothers who became Applebaum, Appleyard and Appletree. In other known cases, occupations became last names: Taylor, Baker, Cook, Miller.

Overall, only 20 percent of all entrants were detained for further examination and, in the end, only two percent were rejected and returned home. For those unfortunate souls, the steamship firms that brought them had to provide return passage.

Aware of the photographer's presence, Captain Leithauser of the *Patricia (above)* strikes an imposing stand during his midday inspection on the bridge. The Captain headed a crew of 249 that looked after 2,489 passengers and six holds of valuable, sometimes precious cargo.

PRINZESSIN VICTORIA LUISE.

The management of Hamburg-America was not simply content with transatlantic first-class or steerage passengers. Long before it became a popular diversion, the company recognized the importance of deluxe, almost yachtlike cruising. Cruises soon gained great popularity, especially the winter runs to the Eastern Mediterranean—then often referred to as "the Orient"—and later the summer excursions to the Northlands—the Baltic, the Norwegian fjords and even as far afield as Spitzbergen.

In 1900, Hamburg-America took delivery of the first passenger ship ever designed exclusively for cruising. In every aspect, she was intended to cater to the very rich. Named *Prinzessin Victoria Luise*, again in deference to the imperial family, she was modeled after the royal yachts of Europe. During his special inspection of the ship, the Kaiser noted that the new vessel was, in fact, larger than his own yacht. However, Hamburg-America included an Imperial Suite on board, which appeased the Kaiser. The other 119 staterooms were also the last word in oceangoing comfort. Each was fitted with a bedroom, private drawing room and full bath.

While her career was highly publicized and led to the creation of more cruising ships, her sailing days were quite brief. In 1906, only six years after completion, she grounded herself at Jamaica during a West Indies cruise and was a total loss. [Built by Blohm & Voss Shipbuilders, Hamburg, Germany, 1900. 4,409 gross tons; 407 feet long; 47 feet wide. Steam quadruple expansion engines geared to twin screw. Service speed 15 knots. Approximately 400 first-class passengers.]

NIEUW AMSTERDAM.
The Holland-America Line tended to be a very conservative firm,
one that attempted to appeal to comfort-seeking first-class passengers as well as those tens of thousands in the profitable steerage sections. When the *Nieuw Amsterdam* was commissioned as
their flagship in the spring of 1906, she followed a very traditional
design with four tall masts that reminded potential passengers of
the great sailing clippers of what was then referred to as "the good
old days." The company even went a step further. The *Nieuw
Amsterdam* carried a full set of sails—the last liner ever to do so.
The ship is shown here, in a rather poetic photo, while docked at
the Holland-America terminal in Hoboken, just across the Hudson from West 12th Street in Manhattan. [Built by Harland &
Wolff Limited, Belfast, Northern Ireland, 1906. 16,967 gross tons;
615 feet long; 68 feet wide. Steam quadruple expansion engines
geared to twin screw. Service speed 16 knots. 2,886 passengers
(440 first class, 246 second, 2,200 third class).]

LA PROVENCE (above).

The upper decks on the early North Atlantic steamers offered little room for strolling passengers. These open areas were cluttered with ventilators, tubes, piping, deckhouses, lifeboats, davits and the casings surrounding the funnels. In this view aboard *La Provence* of the French Line, two gentleman passengers seem somewhat lost in the vast assortment of crowded devices. [Built by Chantiers de Penhoet, Saint-Nazaire, France, 1906. 13,753 gross tons; 627 feet long; 65 feet wide. Steam triple expansion engines geared to twin screw. Service speed 21 knots. 1,362 passengers (422 first class, 132 second class, 808 steerage).]

ESPAGNE (opposite, top).

The French Line—also known as the Compagnie Générale Transatlantique (CGT for short)—did not advance as quickly as the rival British or German Atlantic liner firms. Instead, the French opted for slower, more practical ships that could trade not only on the mail run to New York but also to the colonial West Indian islands of Guadeloupe and Martinique and, on occasion, to Cen-

tral and South America with immigrants. In this scene, the *Espagne* is shown loading passengers and cargo at Saint-Nazaire for a run to Central America. [Built by Ateliers et Chantiers de Provence, Port de Bouc, France, 1910. 11,155 gross tons; 561 feet long; 60 feet wide. Steam quadruple expansion engines geared to twin screw. Service speed 16.5 knots. 488 passengers (296 first class, 106 second class, 86 third class).]

ROCHAMBEAU (opposite, bottom).

French Line's *Rochambeau* was fitted out with larger steerage spaces for more extensive North Atlantic service. On the express mail and passenger run between Le Havre and New York, 274 crew members looked after 2,078 passengers. [Built by Chantiers de Penhoet, Saint-Nazaire, France, 1911. 12,678 gross tons; 598 feet long; 63 feet wide. Steam triple expansion engines geared to twin screw. Service speed 15 knots. 2,078 passengers (428 second class, 200 third class, 1,450 steerage).]

LAPLAND *(opposite, top)*.

The Belgian flag was carried on the transatlantic passenger run by the Red Star Line. Although later acquired by the J. P. Morgan interests and transferred to the British ensign, ships such as the *Lapland* ran a regular service between Antwerp and New York. Again, immigrants were the mainstay. [Built by Harland & Wolff Limited, Belfast, Northern Ireland, 1909. 17,540 gross tons; 620 feet long; 70 feet wide. Steam quadruple expansion engines geared to twin screw. Service speed 17 knots. 2,536 passengers (394 first class, 352 second class, 1,790 third class).]

FREDERIK VIII *(opposite, bottom)*.

Before nationalist companies such as the Norwegian-America Line and Swedish-American Line were created, thousands of immigrants from Scandinavia used the passenger ships of the Danish-flag Scandinavian-American Line in its service between Copenhagen and New York. The flagship of this operation was the *Frederik VIII*, shown departing from New York with the background of a misty skyline that includes the 792-foot Wool-worth Tower, the world's tallest building in 1913. [Built by Vulkan Shipyards, Stettin, Germany, 1913. 11,580 gross tons; 544 feet long; 62 feet wide. Steam triple expansion engines geared to twin screw. Service speed 17 knots. 1,350 passengers (100 first class, 300 second class, 950 third class).]

NEW YORK *(above)*.

The rigors of the North Atlantic showed no partiality. The glass dome skylight on the top deck of the three-funnel *New York*, of the American Line and the first twin-screw express steamer ever built, was smashed on a number of occasions. Furniture and carpets below would be destroyed and stewards would seal off the flooded passenger areas for the remainder of the crossing. [Built by J. & G. Thomson, Clydebank, Scotland, 1888. 10,508 gross tons; 560 feet long; 63 feet wide. Steam triple expansion engines geared to twin screw. Service speed 20 knots. 1,290 passengers (290 first class, 250 second class, 750 steerage).]

ST. LOUIS (above).

The liner *St. Louis* and her sister ship, the *St. Paul*, carried the Stars and Stripes across the North Atlantic for the American Line, running between England and New York. They were smaller and somewhat less luxurious than many of their foreign contemporaries, but had the attraction of their American registry and tone, which appealed to many voyagers, both those in first class and the westbound immigrants in steerage. [Built by William Cramp & Sons Ship & Engine Building Company, Philadelphia, Pennsylvania, 1895. 11,629 gross tons; 554 feet long; 63 feet wide. Steam quadruple expansion engines geared to twin screw. Service speed 19 knots. 1,340 passengers (320 first class, 220 second class, 800 steerage).]

VIRGINIAN (opposite, top).

The Glasgow-based Allan Line produced two noteworthy sister ships in 1905. They were the *Victorian* and the *Virginian*, the first steam-turbine-driven liners on the North Atlantic. Such machinery was considered quite an improvement over the previously used steam-reciprocating systems. The two 10,600-ton sisters were rated very successful. Shortly afterward, Cunard selected such a system for their new *Carmania* of 19,500 tons. More success followed. Within two years, Cunard used such turbines for their new giant speed queens, the *Lusitania* and *Mauretania*, both over 30,000 tons.

The *Virginian* was also one of the very few liners to reach her fiftieth year. After her Allan Line service between Liverpool and Eastern Canada ended, she was sold to the Swedish-American Line and became their *Drottningholm*, from 1920 until 1948. In that year, she joined the Home Lines of Panama, becoming the *Brasil*, then the *Homeland*, before finally being scrapped in Italy in 1955. [Built by Alexander Stephen & Sons Limited, Glasgow, Scotland, 1905. 10,754 gross tons; 538 feet long; 60 feet wide. Steam turbines geared to triple screw. Service speed 18 knots. 1,712 passengers (426 first class, 286 second class, 1,000 third class).]

BURDIGALA (opposite, bottom).

The Compagnie de Navigation Sud-Atlantique provided services from Bordeaux and Marseilles for the French mail and passenger trade to the east coast of South America. One of its largest and most interesting ships was the *Burdigala*, a vessel that had spent 12 years of her life in lay-up. Built in Danzig in 1898 as the *Kaiser Friedrich* of the North German Lloyd, she was intended to be an express liner on the mainline Bremerhaven–New York run. However, after completion, her projected speed was well below expectations and therefore quite unsatisfactory to the Lloyd directors. She went back to the shipyard for further repairs, only to return to service still incapable of her required 22-knot speed. Again she was returned to her builders. A third attempt at operation proved unsuccessful. An international scandal erupted between the North German Lloyd and the Danzig shipyard. In the end, the shipyard was defeated. After a brief charter to the rival Hamburg-America Line, which was equally displeased with the liner's operating performance, she went back to the shipyard and remained there for a full 12 years. When she was finally sold to the French in 1912, she was thoroughly refitted and given new boilers. Only then did she achieve some success. Unfortunately, she survived only a scant four more years. She was sunk in an Aegean mine field in November 1916. [Built by the Schichau Shipyards, Danzig, Germany, 1898. 12,481 gross tons; 600 feet long; 63 feet wide. Steam quadruple expansion engines geared to twin screw. Service speed 19 knots. 1,350 passengers (400 first class, 250 second class, 700 steerage).]

KENILWORTH CASTLE (top).

On the passenger run to South Africa, Britain's Union-Castle Line was unrivaled. The roots of the firm dated back to 1853, when the Union Steam Collier Company ordered five ships to carry coal from South Wales to Southampton for use by the P&O (Peninsular and Oriental Line) and other steamers of the day. The coal run was eventually abandoned, and after a brief, unsuccessful stint in South American shipping, the Union Company received the British Government's mail contract to South Africa in 1857. Success followed. It also encouraged other companies to compete, among them the Castle Mail Packets Company. Thereafter, the competition was brisk, sometimes ferocious and very similar to the situation that then existed on the North Atlantic.

South Africa's mineral wealth was strong reason for heavy passenger loads and consequently bigger ships were built. But by 1900, with competing firms looked upon as inefficient, the South African Government offered a joint mail contract. Both the Union and Castle companies had no choice but to share in the arrangement. Thus, in March of that year, services of the newly merged Union-Castle Mail Steamship Company began. The mainline mail service started at Southampton, and after a stop at either Madeira or Las Palmas, proceeded south to Capetown, Port Elizabeth, East London and Durban. The *Kenilworth Castle* was one of the principal mailships of her day. [Built by Harland & Wolff Limited, Belfast, Northern Ireland, 1903. 12,975 gross tons; 590 feet long; 64 feet wide. Steam quadruple expansion engines geared to twin screw. Service speed 17 knots. 810 passengers (340 first class, 200 second class, 270 third class).]

BALMORAL CASTLE (bottom).

In the age long before air travel, passenger ships provided the means of travel for everyone. In 1910, Union-Castle's mailship *Balmoral Castle* was temporarily reclassified as a royal yacht and used by members of the British royal family, who were traveling to Capetown for the opening of the South African Parliament. [Built by Fairfield Shipbuilding & Engineering Company, Glasgow, Scotland, 1910. 13,361 gross tons; 590 feet long; 64 feet wide. Steam quadruple expansion engines geared to twin screw. Service speed 17 knots. 810 passengers (320 first class, 220 second class, 270 third class).]

NIAGARA.
Not all British-flag liner companies traded directly with the mother country. In addition to its local operations and trade to Australia, the Union Steamship Company of New Zealand operated a transpacific link between Sydney and Vancouver. At the time of the First World War, the steamer *Niagara* was the flagship of this long-distance service. [Built by John Brown & Company Limited, Clydebank, Scotland, 1913. 13,415 gross tons; 543 feet long; 66 feet wide. Steam triple expansion engines geared to triple screw. Service speed 17 knots. 704 passengers (290 first class, 223 second class, 191 third class).]

EMPRESS OF INDIA.

Apart from their transatlantic liners and sizable fleet of inland river and lake steamers, Canadian Pacific maintained a passenger-ship operation on the Pacific. The operations were part of the firm's almost worldwide operation and extended from British Columbia to Japan, Hong Kong and China. Among the earlier ships on this run were three particularly graceful, almost yachtlike vessels that were known as the "Pacific Empresses." Each had an imperial name: *Empress of India* (shown here), *Empress of Japan* and *Empress of China*. [*Empress of India*: Built by the Naval Construction & Armaments Company Limited, Barrow-in-Furness, England, 1891. 5,905 gross tons; 455 feet long; 51 feet wide; 31-foot draft. Steam triple expansion engines geared to twin screw. Service speed 16 knots. 770 passengers (120 first class, 50 second class, 600 steerage).]

SHIPS OF STATE

Those first four-stackers, the early Atlantic greyhounds, were a great and encouraging success. Boardroom discussions called for yet bigger ships. Governments, notably the British and German, were equally as positive. Such major ships not only enhanced the national image but might even be used for military purposes. But the thought of war in the years 1909 and 1910 was very distant. Further support for bigger liners came from the traveling public, from the titled rich in first class to the poorest immigrants in steerage. They loved them. First-class voyagers preferred the distinction, the cachet, of sailing in such enormous vessels. Masses of immigrants still theorized that such ships offered the safest and smoothest ride of their "voyage of a lifetime."

Cunard's *Lusitania* and *Mauretania* (both 1907) were the principal catalysts. As the first turbine-driven superliners, they were both enjoying unparalleled success. White Star, American-owned but operated under the British flag, was Cunard's chief rival on the Liverpool–New York express run. In 1909, White Star decided to retaliate in a dramatic effort. The company would build not two, but three liners that would be the largest and most luxurious afloat: the *Olympic*, *Titanic* and *Gigantic*. But even this ambitious project was soon to be surpassed.

The Germans were determined to show off their industrial might and maritime presence. There was no better way than to have the largest ships afloat. If the *Olympic* and *Titanic*, at 46,000 tons each, were then the biggest, the Hamburg-America Line responded with the 52,000-ton *Imperator*, then with the 54,000-ton *Vaterland* and finally with a 56,000-tonner, the *Bismarck*. From the height of their funnels to the sizes of their lounges and the number of passengers they carried, no trio of ships had ever had such proportions.

In those years of waning peace just prior to the First World War, a near-incredible generation of ocean giants appeared. Even the French produced a new flagship, not distinctive for size or speed but a floating showcase of national art and decor. These were the "ships of state," the magnificent representatives of their country, builders and owners. When they succeeded, as most of them did, it was considered a matter of deep national honor. But when the fates were reversed, as with the tragic maiden-voyage loss of the *Titanic*, it was a sharp wound to national pride.

OLYMPIC.

Britain's White Star Line, the archrival of Cunard and one of the leading firms on the North Atlantic run, was in its prime in the first decade of the twentieth century. Business was booming and the company's ships were growing larger and more luxurious. However, White Star had no ambition toward speed in her liners. Instead, the concentration was on greater size and grander accommodations, with new superships that would outshine almost all others, notably the Cunarders *Lusitania* and *Mauretania*.

With sufficient capital in hand and a promising outlook, White Star ordered no fewer than three mammoth liners. Enticing details were released to an interested public. These would be the first passenger ships to exceed 40,000 tons (the two prides of Cunard were 31,000 tons). Even their name choices hinted at great size: *Gigantic*, *Titanic* and *Olympic*. Internally, they would be the most splendid liners on the Atlantic, each with an Arabian indoor pool (the first ever on transatlantic steamers), first-class staterooms decorated in eleven different schemes and a palm court of lush greenery. In addition to a second and third class, they would be carrying an unparalleled first class of more than 900, the highest yet in that designation. For these three new ocean queens, White Star turned to one of the master shipbuilders of the day, Harland & Wolff at Belfast in Northern Ireland.

On October 20, 1910, the first of the trio was launched as the *Olympic*. But White Star's greatest day came over six months later, on May 31, when the second liner, the *Titanic*, was launched at noon. Then, in the afternoon, invited guests, dignitaries and press boarded the finished *Olympic* for her first run, an overnight cruise to Southampton. The innards of the giant *Olympic* seemed to be her most promising feature. She was sumptuous. To the excited press, she became the first of the "floating palaces."

In the photograph above, taken at the Belfast shipyards in the spring of 1912, two of White Star's three superliners are berthed together. The *Titanic* (left) is fitting out prior to her ill-fated maiden voyage. The *Olympic* (right) is undergoing some repairs. At the time of her maiden voyage from Southampton to New York in June 1911 *(opposite)*, the *Olympic* was heralded as the world's largest liner. Her 45,300-ton record was surpassed a year later by her sister ship the *Titanic*, at 46,300 tons. These highly prized statistics were soon eclipsed by the arrival of the 52,000-ton *Imperator*, the brand-new flagship of Imperial Germany. [*Olympic*: Built by Harland & Wolff Limited, Belfast, Northern Ireland, 1911. 45,324 gross tons; 882 feet long; 92 feet wide; 34-foot draft. Steam triple expansion engines geared to triple screw. Service speed 21 knots. 2,764 passengers (1,054 first class, 510 second class, 1,200 third class).]

The *Olympic*. The decor aboard the *Olympic* and her White Star sisters reflected shoreside themes—palaces, mansions, even Arabian concoctions—and was intended to remind passengers of a hotel on land, as did the lounge shown above. Particularly in first class, White Star attempted to have passengers ignore the sea and the passage itself, transforming the ship into a moving resort.

The following excerpt from a letter posted by a first-class passenger aboard the *Olympic* at sea, dated June 19, 1913, reflects the overall impression of the ship.

> Everything considered, this is the finest boat in the world—not quite so fast as the *Mauretania* and the *Lusitania*, but infinitely more luxurious and more comfortable. The rooms are big and luxuriously furnished, and the restaurant is a model of excellence. It is a better restaurant, service considered and everything considered, than there is in all New York. I hear some complaint about the service in the big dining room down below (second and third class), but I do not know if there is any justification for it.

The verandah *(opposite, top)* provided a setting for leisurely gatherings and the ritual of afternoon tea.

For her first-class passengers, the *Olympic* even provided spa-like facilities, such as the below-deck Turkish bath *(opposite, bottom)*. Adjacent was the Arabian indoor pool, complete with bronze lamps and a marble drinking fountain. A fully equipped gymnasium was also offered the passengers.

Cooling Room, Turkish Bath.

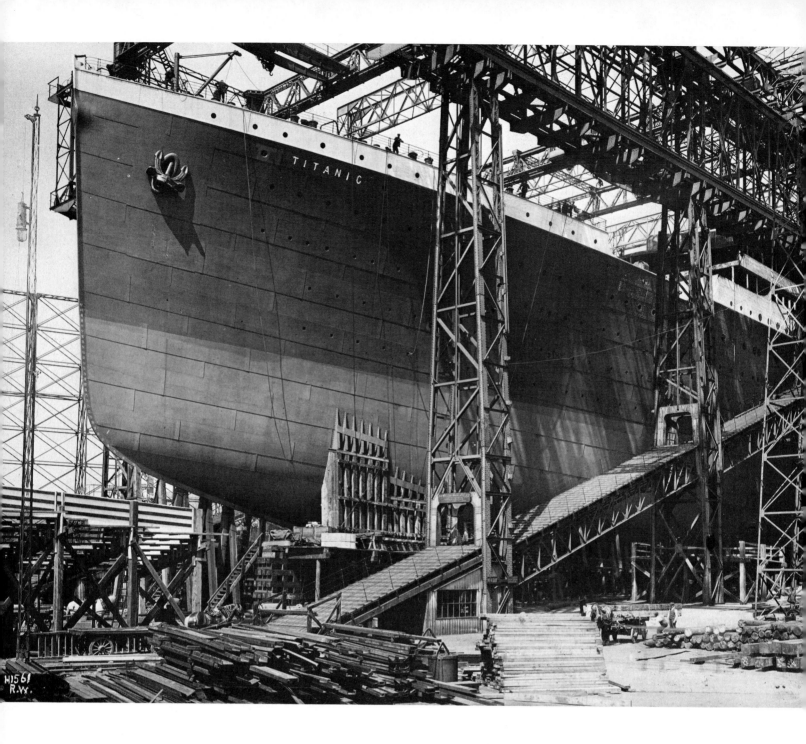

TITANIC.

The White Star Line could never have envisioned the impact of the second superliner on her time and on history. Because of the tragedy of her maiden trip, she has remained the most famous and well-known ship of all time. Over 300 poems and at least 75 different songs—along with a seemingly endless number of books, magazine and newspaper articles, studies, major films and television dramas—have been created about the *Titanic* and her ill-fated inaugural voyage.

Because she was the second of a three-liner set, the company publicists worked doubly hard on creating a separate identity just for her. Thus, even before the maiden voyage, the *Titanic* was a well-known ship. But White Star went a step further, advertising it as the "world's first unsinkable ship." She was fitted with extra watertight compartments and, because of their absolute confidence, there were too few lifeboats and lifesaving gear for her 2,600 passengers and nearly 900 crew members.

She was laid down on March 31, 1909 and was launched with great publicity on May 31, 1911. Like her earlier near-sister *Olympic*, she had four towering funnels, the fourth of which was false and added just for effect. Four stacks conveyed to the traveling public, particularly those in steerage, an overall sense of size, speed, safety and security. After all, despite the tributes to the opulence of her first-class quarters, the *Titanic's* greatest profits would come from those in steerage, those immigrants seeking only westbound passages.

The great hull of the *Titanic* is seen opposite, ready for launching at the Belfast shipyards. After completion, she went on acceptance trials (*above*).

In an exceptionally rare photograph of the *Titanic*, seen docked at Southampton just prior to her maiden departure for New York (*right*), the ship is "dressed overall" with fluttering flags. She rarely flew those traditional flags from end to end.

The maiden crossing of the *Titanic* from Southampton to New York has been very well documented. Suffice it to say that she departed from Southampton on April 10, 1912. In the process, she nearly collided with the American liner *New York*, which to some was a bad omen. Then, just before midnight on the 14th, she side-swiped with an iceberg that ripped a 300-foot-long gash in her starboard side. The cut was fatal and the ship was doomed. Two-and-a-half hours later, at 2:20 A.M., the liner sank in a position 380 miles east of Newfoundland in 12,000 feet of cold North Atlantic water. An estimated 1,522 passengers and crew were lost. At 4:10 A.M., the first rescue ship appeared and began receiving the 705 survivors (or approximately 32 percent of those who had sailed aboard the *Titanic*).

This tragedy was the worst sea disaster to date. The White Star Line never fully recovered. Safety aboard passenger ships was improved. To some, the disaster was so shattering, so demoralizing that it was looked upon as the beginning of the end of the British Empire. [Built by Harland & Wolff Limited, Belfast, Northern Ireland, 1912. 46,329 gross tons; 882 feet long; 92 feet wide; 34-foot draft. Steam triple expansion engines geared to triple screw. Service speed 21 knots. 2,603 passengers (905 first class, 564 second class, 1,134 third class).]

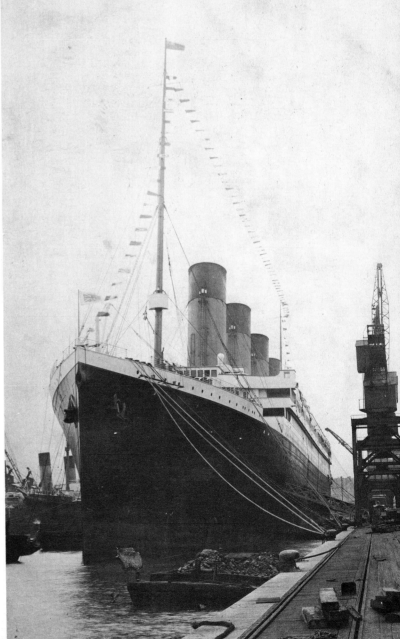

FRANCE.

Since the transatlantic trade was continuing to grow and both the British and Germans were building bigger liners, the French wanted their competitive share as well. In 1909, they ordered a new liner, a member of the prestige four-stacker class, that was twice the size of any previous passenger ship under the tricolor. Although first intended to be named *La Picardie*, she was more appropriately launched as the *France* on September 20, 1910.

She was commissioned in April 1912 and, arriving in New York just two weeks after the *Titanic* disaster, was immediately given high praises. Although hardly the largest or fastest liner on the Atlantic, she was the flagship of the French merchant marine. However, she received greatest attention from her decoration; she was one of the finest liners afloat. In her public rooms and upper-deck staterooms, the *France* offered styles that included Louis XIV, Empire and Moorish. The two-deck-high restaurant in first class featured superb cooking, a distinction that was attached to French liners for decades to come.

As did all other large liners of the day, the *France* balanced her sailings (between Le Havre and New York) with the millionaire set in first-class accommodations (shown, in the bottom view, in the drawing room of a suite), the less affluent in second class and the immigrants in steerage. Overall, she proved a highly successful ship and prompted the French Line to order no fewer than four progressively larger and more extravagant luxury ships. The 34,500-ton *Paris* was next in the master plan. [Built by Chantiers de Penhoet, Saint-Nazaire, France, 1912. 23,666 gross tons; 713 feet long; 75 feet wide. Steam turbines geared to quadruple screw. Service speed 24 knots. 2,026 passengers (534 first class, 442 second class, 250 third class, 800 steerage).]

IMPERATOR.

The Germans, represented by the Hamburg-America Line, wanted to surpass the British. It was not simply a case of corporate rivalry but one of national prestige. Cunard had the speed queens *Lusitania* and *Mauretania*, and were planning a third major ship, the *Aquitania*; White Star had a three-ship plan of its own—the *Olympic*, *Titanic* and *Britannic* (planned as the *Gigantic*); the Hamburg-America offices responded with a trio of liners that would be the largest and most extravagant ships ever seen. The keel plates for the first, talked of as "the colossus" of the Atlantic, were put in place on June 18, 1910. The 46,000-ton White Star sisters *Olympic* and *Titanic* were under construction at the same time at Belfast. A few months later, Cunard ordered the *Aquitania*, also near 46,000 tons. At best estimates, the new German liner would be over 52,000 tons. The race had begun. (None of these liners was ever intended to be in the Blue Ribband class. Record speed was left to Cunard's *Mauretania*, which was the fastest on the Atlantic from 1907 until 1929. These ships competed for the distinctions of largest and grandest.)

Hamburg-America selected a three-stack design for their giant new flagship. In fact, rising 69 feet above the upper deck, these

funnels were among the largest ever fitted to a liner. (Later they would create balance problems and were cut down by nine feet.) Two masts towered at both ends of the ship. Along her decks were 83 lifeboats and two motor launches (figures prompted by the *Titanic* tragedy), four four-bladed propellers that could make 185 revolutions per minute and twin engine rooms that were 69 and 95 feet long and had bunkers for 8,500 tons of coal.

In a bid to transcend national boundaries and attract more passengers, the liner was to be named *Europa*. However, the German Kaiser, Wilhelm II, became so fascinated and excited with the new ship, it seemed more fitting to name her *Imperator*. The Kaiser launched the new Imperial flagship on May 23, 1912, a mere five weeks after the shock of the *Titanic* sinking. Dressed in an admiral's uniform, the Kaiser climbed to the top of a specially erected platform to do the honors *(opposite, bottom)*. He shared the platform position with Albert Ballin, the genius director of the Hamburg-America Line, who had conceived of the grand three-liner plan. Unfortunately, just prior to the actual christening, a piece of lumber fell from the ship's bow and nearly hit the Kaiser.

As the biggest ship yet created, the *Imperator* was symbolic of Imperial Germany's new technological abilities. The shipyard officials presented the Kaiser with a three-foot-long detailed model of the liner, done completely in silver. The Kaiser, delighted with the overall accomplishment, in turn presented the model to Ballin.

The *Imperator* was completed in the late spring of 1913. She left Cuxhaven (Hamburg) on June 13 for her trip to New York via Southampton. The otherwise festive and triumphant occasion was marked by one very serious blemish: she was top-heavy. She rolled terribly, even in the calmest seas—a fault that could ruin her financially. Therefore, in her first annual overhaul, her three funnels were cut down *(above)*, all upper-deck panels and fittings were replaced by ones done in lighter materials, and a substantial amount of cement was poured along her bottom. To some extent, her rolling was curtailed. Now the Germans looked to the second of the Hamburg-America giants. [Built by Bremer Vulkan Shipyards, Hamburg, Germany, 1913. 52,117 gross tons; 919 feet long; 98 feet wide; 35-foot draft. Steam turbines geared to quadruple screw. Service speed 23 knots. 4,594 passengers (908 first class, 972 second class, 942 third class, 1,772 steerage).]

The *Imperator*. The ship was of immense proportions. Her bow seemed more impressive because of its unique gilt figurehead *(above)* which depicted an eagle, its wings outstretched and a globe clutched in its talons. The globe carried the Hamburg-America motto: "Mein Feld ist die Welt" (the world is my scope). But this unusual ornament was short-lived. Its wings were broken off during one of the liner's early encounters with an Atlantic storm. The eagle was soon removed, and was never replaced.

The *Imperator* was designed to carry more passengers than any other liner afloat. Ignoring the possibilities of the onset of war, the Hamburg-America Line and in particular Albert Ballin saw only the best times ahead. The number of first-class travelers was increasing, and immigration to America was equally as promising (nearly one million crossed to New York in 1914 alone). The *Imperator* and her two intended near-sisters were expected to profit from this prosperity. Teutonic splendors on the North Atlantic *(opposite, top)*: the captain's table in the first-class restaurant aboard the *Imperator*.

An inspection team posed *(opposite, bottom)* in the *Imperator*'s Social Hall. At the far end of the room is a white marble bust of Kaiser Wilhelm, the liner's sponsor at launching, and overhead is an ornate skylight.

The *Imperator*. The *Imperator's* first-class indoor swimming pool *(above)* was one of her most notable amenities. Known as the Pompeian Bath, it was styled after a slightly smaller creation at the Royal Automobile Club in London. Made of marble and with an upper deck spectator's gallery, it was the most sensational facility of its kind ever to go to sea. Even shipboard, the German predilection for health and physical fitness persisted. The ship's gymnasium facilities *(below)* included any number of devices that supposedly toned muscles, shed pounds, stimulated the system.

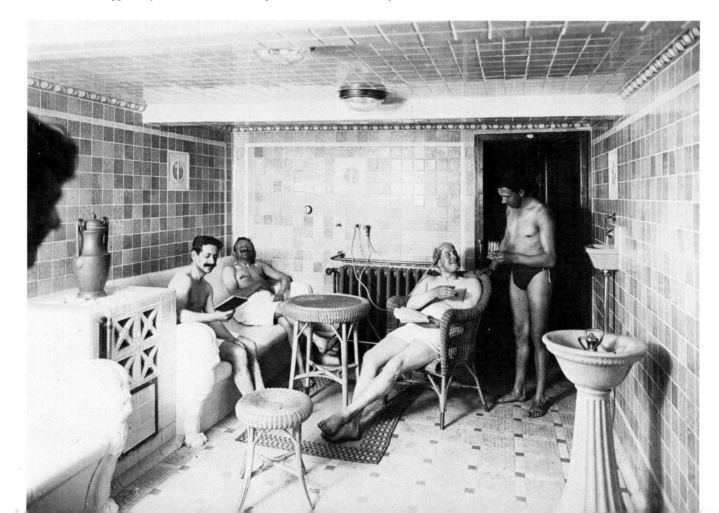

The Imperator. A view taken aboard the ship *(above)* shows a section of the first-class kitchen. At rock bottom of the traveling social hierarchy aboard the *Imperator* were the steerage passengers. Most were Germans, but others represented Eastern European countries. Steerage deck space was limited and included cramped areas in the liner's bow, just beneath her forward mast. The steerage dining area *(below)* was in the forward section. This was hardly desirable. First class had its restaurant amidships (center) and therefore encountered far less movement of the ship. The steerage quarters were bare: exposed steel bulkheads, ceilings and floors, naked lightbulbs, long benches rather than chairs, and rows of tables placed tightly together.

The *Imperator* *(above)*. As a result of the *Titanic* disaster, liner companies developed more extensive and more rigidly enforced safety standards. A variety of the *Imperator's* crew members is lined along the boat deck for muster. All of the liner's 83 lifeboats and davits were frequently tested, which included lowering them into the waters of both New York and Hamburg harbors.

AQUITANIA *(opposite)*.

The third liner ordered by the Cunard Line to complete its weekly express service between Liverpool and New York was never intended to be as fast as either the *Lusitania* or the *Mauretania*. Instead, she was a larger version of their four-stacker design, but, far more importantly, the brand new *Aquitania* of the spring of 1914 was considered one of the most beautifully decorated liners ever to go to sea.

Named after the ancient Roman province in southwest France, she was almost immediately nicknamed "the ship beautiful." The grace of her design and beauty of her accommodations became

legendary. Cunard was immediately assured of a most successful ship. To some, there were no finer rooms afloat than the *Aquitania's* Caroline smoking room, her Palladian lounge and her Louis XVI restaurant. There were also the Adam drawing room, the Jacobean grill room and an indoor pool decorated with replicas of Egyptian ornaments in the British Museum.

The *Aquitania* was the last of the new Atlantic four-stackers (only two more such ships were built but for the South African trade of the Union-Castle Line). In fact, the Cunarder was the very last four-stack ship to remain in use, being retired in 1949, after 35 years of service. She was quite similar to Germany's giant *Vaterland* in that both ships were completed just before the outbreak of the First World War and consequently saw only brief commercial service at first. [Built by John Brown & Company Limited, Clydebank, Scotland, 1914. 45,647 gross tons; 901 feet long; 97 feet wide. Steam turbines geared to quadruple screw. Service speed 23 knots. 3,230 passengers (618 first class, 614 second class, 1,998 third class).]

The *Aquitania*. For more secluded, specialty first-class dining, the *Aquitania* offered a Jacobean grill room *(top)*. An extra fee was charged for the privilege of admittance.

The two-deck-high Louis XVI restaurant in first class *(middle)* was considered one of the *Aquitania*'s finest rooms. Some of the chairs were saved when the liner was scrapped in 1950. After some refinishing and reupholstering, they were used in the first-class restaurant of another Cunarder, the 22,000-ton *Carinthia*, commissioned in 1957. After that ship was withdrawn in 1968, the history of those chairs is unclear.

Palm courts, winter gardens, veranda lounges and garden lounges *(bottom)* were very much in style for ocean liners, particularly in the decade prior to the First World War.

A poetic photo *(opposite)* captures the *Aquitania* as she sails from Cunard's New York terminal at Pier 54, West 12th Street.

VATERLAND.

If Hamburg-America's *Imperator* was the biggest ship in the world in 1913 (at 52,100 tons), the second of the German giants was bigger still. This new ship was, at best estimations, expected to exceed 54,000 tons. Again, the Germans would surely have the world's largest ship.

The original plan was to name her *Europa*, again in an attempt to capture more of a general European market, but in the end nationalism prevailed. She was named *Vaterland*, on April 3, 1913, by Prince Rupert of Bavaria. One of the oddities about the three great German superliners was that their christening, in contrast to tradition, was done by men. The Kaiser had done the honors for the *Imperator*, Prince Rupert did the *Vaterland* and, on the occasion of the last launching, that of the *Bismarck*, the Kaiser unexpectedly did the job after the intended sponsor, Countess Hanna von Bismarck, had muffed it. The launching was a carefully planned affair. Once waterborne *(above)* the 950-foot long hull had to be almost immediately stopped for fear of ramming the opposite bank of the Elbe River.

Some 40,000 people attended the Hamburg launching of the *Vaterland (opposite)*. She was yet another German liner of wonders. 1.5 million rivets were used in her construction. The ship's bunkers held 9,000 tons of coal and there was space for 12,000 tons of cargo. The 1,180-member crew was headed by a commodore, four assistant captains, seven nautical officers and 29 engineers.

For transatlantic luxury, she was in the top class. The accommodations in first class included a winter garden, social hall, large dining salon, grill room and smoking room. There was an entire row of shops, a bank, a travel bureau and an indoor pool-gymnasium complex. There were 752 beds in the first-class staterooms, headed by two extremely luxurious imperial suites and ten deluxe apartments. Each consisted of a bedroom, sitting room and marble bath. [Built by Blohm & Voss Shipbuilders, Hamburg, Germany, 1914. 54,282 gross tons; 950 feet long; 100 feet wide; 35-foot draft. Steam turbines geared to quadruple screw. Service speed 23 knots. 3,909 passengers (752 first class, 535 second class, 850 third class, 1,772 steerage).]

The _Vaterland_. Work progressed on outfitting the ship _(opposite, top)_. Once she was completed (in the spring of 1914), publicists emphasized the strength and safety of her construction. Much had been learned from the _Titanic_ disaster and from the balance problems encountered with the _Imperator_. Among the _Vaterland_'s more outstanding features was a full wireless telegraph system that was manned around-the-clock, strengthened hull plating and decking, a huge searchlight on the foremast (presumably to spot icebergs, among other objects) and the finest fire prevention system then afloat. However, commercial life for the world's largest ship was quite brief. She left Hamburg on her maiden crossing to New York on May 14, 1914. In August, she was interned at New York when war erupted.

Early in the summer of 1914, at Cowes on the English south coast, the Germans had the opportunity to note their startling technological progress _(opposite, bottom)_. The four-masted _Kaiserin Auguste Victoria_ (left) had been the largest ship afloat in 1906, at 24,500 tons and 705 feet. The _Vaterland_ (right) had just succeeded to that prized position, measuring over 54,200 tons and 950 feet. Glorying in British envy, the Germans were beaming. However, in a matter of a few short years, it was all to change. After the German defeat in the First World War, the _Kaiserin Auguste Victoria_ hoisted the British colors and became the _Empress of Scotland_ for Canadian Pacific. Even more agonizing to her builders and former Hamburg owners, the _Vaterland_ was taken by the United States as a war prize and became the _Leviathan_, the largest vessel yet to fly the Stars and Stripes.

The _Vaterland_'s first-class dining salon _(right, top)_ was somewhat more refined than those in some of the other Atlantic sea queens. The simple beauty of the room was enhanced by the spectacular circular ceiling mural, which was surrounded by glowing lamps. In a view, taken at dinnertime during a crossing to New York _(right, middle)_, the same room does not seem quite as large when filled with passengers.

Long, leisurely evenings were spent on board liners like the _Vaterland_ in the quiet comfort of smoking rooms _(right, bottom)_ and palm courts. Life, at least for the first-class passengers, was almost tranquilizing. Although there might be a concert or a dance band, it was an age long before ships featured masquerade balls, first-run films and stand-up comics.

BISMARCK.

The Germans were never able to enjoy the third and largest of their supertrio, the "Big Three" as they became known. Many saw a bad omen even in the launching on June 20, 1914 *(above)*. Countess Hanna von Bismarck, granddaughter of the famed German chancellor, was to do the christening honors, but when she released the ceremonial bottle of wine, it missed its intended target. The Kaiser, who was standing alongside the young Countess, stepped forward and christened the ship instead. Eight days later, the gunshots at Sarajevo shattered world peace. Archduke Ferdinand had been killed, an event leading to the First World War. The *Bismarck* was never to sail for her German owners.

Throughout the war, the *Bismarck* sat at her builder's yard, a rusting shell of what was intended to be the world's largest ship and flagship of the German merchant fleet. It had been rumored that the liner would be completed and would be used to carry the Kaiser and the entire Imperial Family on an around-the-world victory cruise. Instead, in 1919, the Kaiser was in exile following Germany's defeat. Albert Ballin, the guiding genius of Hamburg-America and the "Big Three," was so shattered that he took his own life. Surviving Germans hoped that the liner would be completed to reactivate national service. The victorious Allies had other plans.

It was a bitter decision to the Germans, especially to the Hamburg shipbuilders, that the Treaty of Versailles gave the *Bismarck* to the British as reparation for the loss of White Star's 48,000-ton *Britannic*, mined in 1916. Reluctantly, shipyard crews began the task of completing the liner, but to British specifications.

Construction was delayed by deliberate slowness on the part of the German work crews and by shortages of steel in postwar Germany. There was also a fire at the yard in October 1920. When staff members from the White Star Line, the new owners of the ship, arrived at Hamburg in March 1922 to take delivery of the completed vessel, they were shocked to find the name *Bismarck* clearly painted on the bow and her funnels in Hamburg-America colors. The new British master even found his cabin being used as a storage closet. The Germans were reluctant to the very end to see the giant liner depart *(left)*. She sailed for the Irish Sea for her trials and was formally renamed *Majestic*, repainted with White Star funnel colors and relisted with Liverpool as her homeport. [Built by Blohm & Voss Shipbuilders, Hamburg, Germany, 1914–22. 56,551 gross tons; 956 feet long; 100 feet wide; 35-foot draft. Steam turbines geared to quadruple screw. Service speed 23.5 knots. Intended capacity of over 3,500 passengers in first, second and third classes and in steerage. Exact figures per class never determined.]

BRITANNIC.

The third of the White Star Line's trio of luxurious express liners was intended to be named *Gigantic*. However, on the heels of the *Titanic* disaster, a name alluding to grandiose proportions was considered unwise. Instead, the name *Britannic* was selected. However, the career of this major liner is perhaps the most pathetic of any. She was in service for just a year and never made a commercial sailing. Launched on February 26, 1914, her completion was halted by the outbreak of war in August. In November 1915, under orders from the British Admiralty, she was finished as a hospital ship. A year later, on November 21, while on duty in the Aegean, she ran into a German mine, exploded and sank with the loss of 21 lives. The *Britannic* was one of the least-known big ships of her time. Along with the loss of the *Titanic*, her demise was to signal further the slow decline of the once great White Star Company.

The *Britannic* was fitted with a series of exceptionally large, almost crane-like davits that could, in an emergency, launch a series of lifeboats. Although ungainly in respect to the liner's otherwise pleasant, gently relaxed profile, such units were obviously safety mechanisms added following the *Titanic's* sinking. [Built by Harland & Wolff Limited, Belfast, Northern Ireland, 1914–15. 48,158 gross tons; 903 feet long; 94 feet wide. Steam triple expansion engines geared to triple screw. Service speed 21 knots. 2,573 passengers (790 first class, 830 second class, 953 third class).]

THE GREAT WAR

In that fateful summer of 1914, the dramatic events following the assassination of the Austrian archduke pitted Imperial Germany in war against Britain, France and Russia. Passenger shipping on all seas, and especially on the North Atlantic, was immediately affected. Most commercial trading came to a screeching halt.

In August 1914, in a flash of orders, the *Mauretania* sped to refuge in Halifax, while the *Olympic* sought the safety of New York. The *Kronprinzessin Cecilie* put into Bar Harbor, disguised as the *Olympic* no less. Soon European liners—both large and small—were called to duty, some as armed merchant cruisers, others as troopers and still others as hospital ships. Dazzle-painting, in grays, blacks and blues, overlaid the former peacetime colors and confused the identity of many ships, especially to the predatory U-boat crews. Ships went to distant waters, all under military orders. The likes of the giant *Aquitania* and *Olympic* appeared in the distant waters of the Aegean on medical duty. The *Aquitania's* splendid Palladian lounge was suddenly a hospital ward.

The losses were staggering. From the start, the Germans lost over 30 ships that were caught in American ports when war was declared. Among these were the *Vaterland*, the world's largest liner, and such other notables as the *Amerika, Kaiser Wilhelm II* and *George Washington*. But far more dramatic and shocking was the loss of Cunard's *Lusitania,* torpedoed by an enemy U-boat off Ireland on May 7, 1915. Some 1,198 perished, 159 of whom were Americans. Mark Sullivan, one of the noted historians of the time, wrote: "That was the precise day . . . when war between America and Germany became inevitable." By April 1917, the United States had joined the Allies against the Kaiser's forces. Those interned German liners, including the *Vaterland,* which became the U.S.S. *Leviathan,* were now working against the country that had created them.

By the war's end in November 1918, worldwide shipping was completely changed. The British alone had lost 1,169 ships. Notably, Cunard had lost one express liner, the *Lusitania,* while White Star's *Britannic* was gone as well, sunk less than a year after her completion. The Armistice had stripped Germany of almost all of her liners, including the trio of giants *Imperator, Vaterland* and *Bismarck.* The Hamburg-America Line, which in 1913 had the largest passenger fleet on the Atlantic as well as the world's largest liner, was left only with the *Deutschland.* Still mechanically faulty, with two stacks instead of her original four, she reopened her owner's postwar service as an all-immigrant ship.

KAISER WILHELM DER GROSSE (opposite, top).

In August 1914, the German liner companies canceled all sailings. War had begun. Some German ships were fortunate to be in German waters or nearby. Others were either captured or interned, such as the 30 or so ships caught in American ports. The *Kaiser Wilhelm der Grosse* was taken at Bremen by the Imperial German Navy for conversion to a high-speed armed merchant cruiser. Her mission: raids on Allied commercial shipping. Once in the North Atlantic, she sank three ships and stopped two British passenger liners for military inspection. On August 26, at Rio de Oro in Spanish West Africa, the former liner was bunkering when the British cruiser H.M.S. *Highflyer* appeared. A duel between the two ships followed. When the *Kaiser Wilhelm der Grosse* had exhausted her ammunition supplies, her captain ordered the ship to be scuttled with explosives. The first big German liner was lost in action.

KRONPRINZESSIN CECILIE (opposite, bottom).

Another German superliner, the *Kronprinzessin Cecilie*, was at sea off the North American coast on July 29, 1914, when word was received that war in Europe was imminent. Her position was worrisome. She was carrying not only some German passengers, but also a precious cargo of $10 million in gold bars and $1 million in silver destined for Bremerhaven. The captain realized that safe passage, without capture by the British, was impossible. Instead, he and his officers devised a dramatic alternative. The ship's lights and wireless were extinguished. Some passengers were furious with this escapade. Others were delighted to be a part of the mysterious manuevers. Still others, a third group, offered to buy the ship so that she could hoist the American flag and sail safely for neutral waters.

Crewmen repainted the tops of the four stacks in White Star colors, with a black band at top and buff coloring beneath. At a distance, the German *Kronprinzessin Cecilie* could be mistaken for the British *Olympic*. The liner reversed course and headed for the safety and solitude of Bar Harbor, Maine. When the German "treasure ship" arrived in the tiny port, locals were astounded to see "the *Olympic*" anchored offshore. News was flashed to New

York, but with a reply that the White Star *Olympic* was, in fact, berthed safely at her Manhattan slip. The true identity of the big liner in Maine was soon uncovered. Although she was interned by the Americans, the escape from the British had worked.

The ship was later moved to Boston to await her fate. The Custom House Tower rises above the liner's second funnel in this view. She sat unused for months. Two of the other five German four-stackers were also in American hands. The *Kaiser Wilhelm II* had been caught at the North German Lloyd piers in Hoboken when war first erupted. She remained there for nearly three years before becoming the U.S. Navy troop-transport U.S.S. *Agamemnon*. The *Kronprinz Wilhelm* spent the earliest months of the war as an armed merchant cruiser. A ship that was built for a luxurious, peaceful service, she sank over 15 Allied ships (a total of over 60,000 tons) in the Atlantic. In April 1915, she put into Newport News, Virginia in an exhausted state. She had no provisions or fuel and was in serious need of repairs. On April 26, she was officially interned by U.S. authorities. Later, upon America's entry into the war in 1917, she was outfitted as a trooper under the name U.S.S. *Von Steuben*.

VATERLAND (above).

One of the worst miscalculations of the German war campaign was to have the giant *Vaterland*, the Imperial flagship and the largest liner afloat, caught at a Hoboken pier when war was declared. For nearly three years the ship sat, rusting and neglected, abandoned in a political limbo. Early in the war, she was used by the German-American community for fund-raising banquets and balls, the profits of which were sent to the Fatherland to support the Kaiser's armies. Then, as America became more seriously threatened by the fighting in Europe, the *Vaterland* became "restricted territory." A small number of her former German crew looked after the otherwise silent ship.

The *Vaterland* was officially seized by America in July 1917. Thereafter, she would be known as the *Leviathan*, flying the Stars and Stripes.

LUSITANIA (opposite, top).

The loss of Cunard's *Lusitania* is surely the most famous ship tragedy of the First World War. Unlike her sister *Mauretania* and the other superliners of the time, the *Lusitania* remained in something of regular wartime service. She operated alone, on monthly sailings between New York and Liverpool, beginning in the summer of 1914 and well into 1915. Initially, there had been some thought given to converting her to an armed merchant cruiser, but this never came to pass. On all of her wartime sailings, some cargo space was reserved for American materials bound for Britain. The official manifest on the fatal sailing, in May 1915, included sheet brass, copper, cheese, beef, barrels of oysters and crates of chicken. But unofficially, there was a far more ominous cargo: 4,200 cases of small-caliber rifle ammunition, 100 cases of shrapnel shells and 18 cases of fuses. Some historians contend that the ship also had ten tons of explosives onboard as well as six million rounds of ammunition and 323 bales of "raw furs," a volatile type of gun cotton that exploded when brought into contact with water.

The *Lusitania* was believed to be too fast for U-boats and, as a passenger ship, immune from attack. However, the first torpedo hit at 2:08 in the afternoon of May 7. Fired from German U-Boat 20, it pierced the *Lusitania's* steel hull under the starboard bridge. A column of steam and water sprayed 160 feet into the air, carrying with it coal, wood and steel splinters. The ship immediately began to flood, taking a 15-degree list from the start. Then there was a second explosion that caused great damage to the bow. Some survivors maintained that this second blast was not the boilers exploding but "the secret, mysterious cargo" as it was hit with seawater. The *Lusitania* sank off Ireland's Old Head of Kinsale 18 minutes after the first hit.

At the time of the tragedy, the *Lusitania* was carrying 1,959 passengers. She had lifesaving gear and lifeboats for 2,605. However, the great list that the ship took almost immediately after the torpedo hit made it impossible to use many of the lifeboats. Furthermore, only six of the ship's 48 boats had stayed afloat. As the *Lusitania's* stern section lifted out of the sea, her propellers were still turning and at least two passengers were sucked into the funnels as they dipped below the water and then were shot outward again when a boiler exploded.

Some 1,198 perished, of whom 758 were passengers. Of the 159 Americans on board, 124 were lost; of 129 children, 94 were dead; and of 35 babies, 31 were missing.

One seaman, Frank Tower, survived with remarkable luck. He had also survived the sinking of the *Titanic* in 1912 and of the *Empress of Ireland* in 1914.

This scene shows five of the *Lusitania's* remaining lifeboats at Queenstown, following the tragedy.

ORMONDE (opposite, bottom).

Noted marine artist Norman Wilkinson headed a British project that fostered the use, especially on the big troopships, of dazzle paint—a system of geometric shapes and angles, done in grays, blacks, whites and dark blues, that was intended to hinder ship-spotting and identification, especially by German U-boat crews. To some extent, it succeeded. The construction of the Orient Line's *Ormonde* halted in 1914, just as the war started; she was completed in 1918 as a troopship. For her maiden voyage, she was dressed in dazzle paint. [Built by John Brown & Company Limited, Clydebank, Scotland, 1913–18. 14,853 gross tons; 600 feet long; 66 feet wide. Steam turbines geared to twin screw. Service speed 18 knots. 1,473 passengers in peacetime (278 first class, 195 second class, 1,000 third class).]

EMPRESS OF RUSSIA (above).

Canadian Pacific's *Empress of Russia* also used dazzle paint on her trooping voyages. To some, the painted effects resembled the teeth of a large sea serpent. The voyages of the liners were often made in great secrecy, without night lights and on zigzagging courses. [Built by Fairfield Shipbuilding & Engineering Company, Glasgow, Scotland, 1913. 16,810 gross tons; 592 feet long; 68 feet wide. Steam turbines geared to quadruple screw. Service speed 20 knots. 1,192 passengers in peacetime (284 first class, 100 second class, 808 Asiatic steerage).]

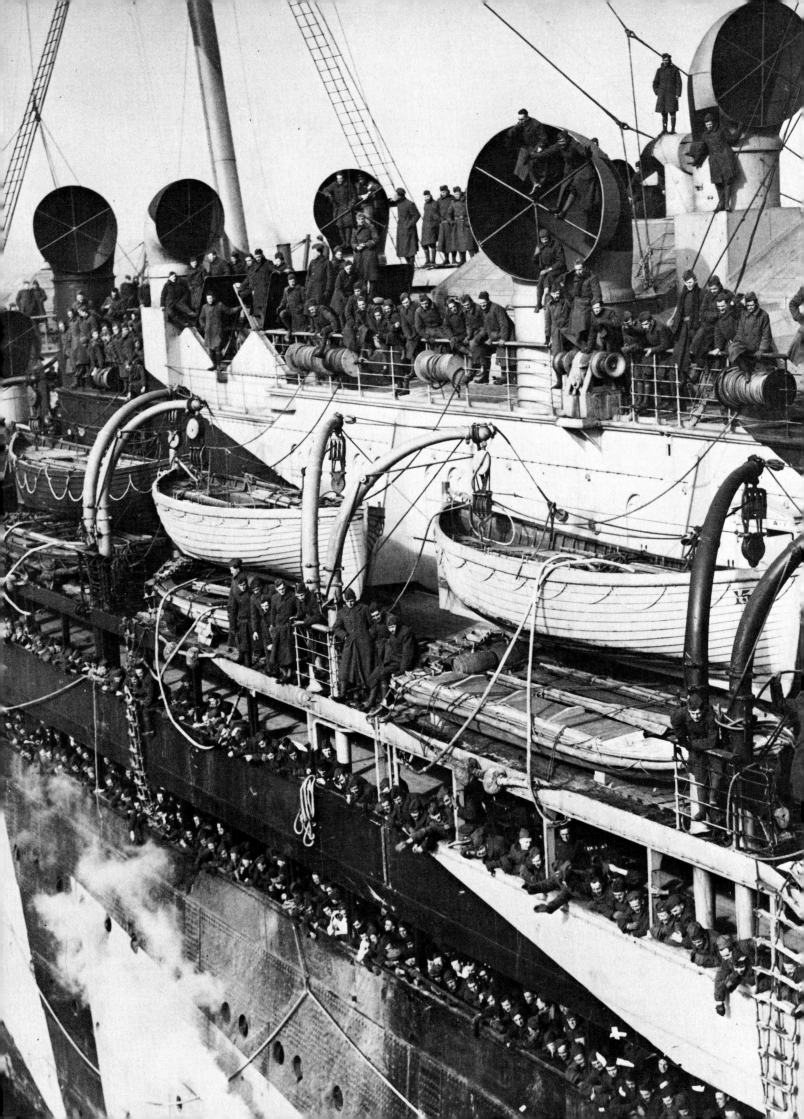

MAURETANIA *(opposite)*.

Cunard's *Mauretania*, the fastest liner afloat, was also repainted in the dazzle effect. She served throughout the war, both as a hospital ship and a trooper. On medical duty, she sailed to the Mediterranean for the Gallipoli campaign. As a troopship, she worked the North Atlantic, carrying tens of thousands of American doughboys to the trenches of Western Europe. Just as she had with her passengers in peacetime days, she endeared herself to the servicemen (here Europe-bound Americans in 1917) who sailed her. To them, she was affectionately known as "the Maury."

ANDANIA *(above)*.

Because of the war, many passenger ships had shortened, often quite brief sailing lives. Cunard's *Andania*, shown here, was commissioned in 1913, for the run between Liverpool and Montreal. A year later, she was requisitioned and converted for trooping duties. In January 1918, a little over four years after her completion, she was torpedoed by a German U-boat. Even more pathetic was the case of Holland-America's 32,200-ton *Statendam*, the new Dutch national flagship being built at Belfast in 1914. She was not completed until 1917, when, because of the lingering hostilities, she was given to the British Government and completed as a trooper called *Justicia*. A year later, on July 19, 1918, she was torpedoed and lost during a voyage to New York. At the war's end, the British gave 60,000 tons of shipbuilding steel to the Holland-America Line in compensation. [Built by Scott's Shipbuilding & Engineering Company Limited, Greenock, Scotland, 1913. 13,405 gross tons; 540 feet long; 64 feet wide. Steam quadruple expansion engines geared to twin screw. Service speed 14.5 knots. 2,140 passengers (520 first class, 1,620 third class).]

FRANCE (opposite, top).

During the war years, the *France* was renamed *France IV*. In 1914, she was converted to a trooper and sent to the Mediterranean campaign. In November 1915, during a major refitting at Toulon, she was converted to a hospital ship, complete with white hull, a bold red stripe and vivid Red Cross markings, some of which could be illuminated for nighttime sailing. Her once-lavish lounges were converted to medical wards. There were also a fully equipped surgery and pharmacy. The doctors and nurses used the former passenger cabins, some of which were occupied by the military wounded. In 1919, the war over, the *France* was returned to the French Line and resumed her luxury service between Le Havre and New York.

STOCKHOLM (opposite, bottom).

Some liner firms, notably the Scandinavian ones, attempted to maintain a commercial service during some of the war years. When the Swedish-American Line first began passenger sailings in 1915, they used a northern course between Gothenburg and New York. Their ships rounded the top of Scotland, passed below Iceland and then clung to the Canadian coastline before reaching the United States.

One of the first Swedish-American liners was the former *Potsdam*, owned by the Holland-America Line. Noted for her exceptionally large single stack, she was often referred to as the "Funneldam." Once in Swedish service by 1915, she was renamed the *Stockholm*, the first of several liners to bear that name. Through a series of cautious passages and periodic lay-ups, she survived the First World War, only to become a victim of the second world conflict. When she was sold by the Swedes in 1929, she was rebuilt as a whaling mother ship. This diverse activity ended when she was captured by the Nazis while sailing in the Antarctic. Returned to Europe, she was finally scuttled at Cher-

bourg in 1944 during the German retreat. A few years later, she was scrapped in England. [Built by Blohm & Voss Shipbuilders, Hamburg, Germany, 1900. 12,835 gross tons; 571 feet long; 62 feet wide. Steam triple expansion engines geared to twin screw. Service speed 15 knots. 2,292 passengers (282 first class, 210 second class, 1,800 steerage).]

CAP POLONIO (above).

The war confused the plans of shipowners. Hamburg–South America Line's *Cap Polonio* was launched in March 1914, intended as the company's new flagship on the run between Hamburg, Rio and Buenos Aires. When the war erupted in the following summer, her construction was halted and she was revised for use as an auxiliary cruiser. With her third stack missing as a form of disguise, she was commissioned in the winter of 1915 as the *Vineta*. She soon proved unsatisfactory, mostly because of her slow passenger-ship speed of only 17 knots. She was then completed as a passenger ship, reverting to her originally intended name, but only to be handed over to Britain as reparations in 1919. Both the Union-Castle and P&O lines each had a turn at running her as a passenger ship but her faulty engines severely handicapped her. In 1921, she was sold back to her original German owners and was thoroughly rebuilt with new machinery. Recommissioned in February 1922 as the *Cap Polonio*, she served a full decade as a highly popular, profitmaking liner. When she was scrapped at Bremerhaven in 1935, her high reputation still remained and some of her furnishings were sold for use by a local hotel. [Built by Blohm & Voss Shipbuilders, Hamburg, Germany, 1914. 20,576 gross tons; 662 feet long; 72 feet wide. Steam triple expansion engines geared to triple screw. Service speed 17 knots. 1,555 passengers (356 first class, 250 second class, 949 third class).]

LEVIATHAN (*VATERLAND*).

Beginning in the summer of 1917 and lasting until the war's end, the former German *Vaterland*, renamed as the American *Leviathan* *(opposite, bottom)*, sailed on the North Atlantic troop shuttle. Such giant troopships needed large staffs; the *Leviathan* was manned by the U.S. Navy *(opposite, top)*. In 1918 she carried General Pershing *(above)*. The general salutes while, behind him with arm raised, is the young Douglas MacArthur.

The *Leviathan*. Following strenuous war service, many of the
ex-German liners that had been seized endured long periods of
uncertainty and indecision. The *Leviathan* sat at her Hoboken pier
for several years *(above)*, neglected as Washington officials decided upon her future. After long and serious deliberation, it was
proposed that she be transferred to the newly formed United
States Lines to become the commercial flagship of the U.S. fleet.
In 1921, she was sent to the Newport News Shipyards in Virginia
for a major refit and conversion. To the dockers at the shipyard,
she looked at first a sorry sight. Restoring the ship to something
of her prewar splendor was no simple task. It required thousands
of workers, plying their crafts throughout the ship *(opposite)*.
Electrical wiring had to be replaced, piping redone, steel reinforced, engines restored and the accommodations for passengers
and crew upgraded completely. Slowly, the *Leviathan* again began
to resemble a great liner. The war was becoming a more distant
memory.

GEORGE WASHINGTON *(top).*
Among the exiled German liners interned at Hoboken in August 1914 was North German Lloyd's *George Washington.* Her American name was a marketing attempt to lure more westbound immigrants on board. The "Big George," as she was affectionately known, remained at her Hoboken pier for nearly three years, until called to duty in April 1917. For the U.S. Navy, she was reconditioned as the U.S.S. *George Washington* and began sailing on the military shuttle between Hoboken and Northern Europe. She was an endearing, well-run ship. Because of this popularity, she was selected to carry President Woodrow Wilson and his party to and from the Peace Conference at Versailles in 1919. The President departed in March and returned in August. Then, with her military duties completed, she passed into the hands of the United States Lines for commercial Atlantic sailings. Despite her German origin, she retained her original name. [Built by Vulkan Shipyards, Stettin, Germany, 1909. 25,570 gross tons; 723 feet long; 72 feet wide. Steam quadruple expansion engines geared to twin screw. Service speed 18.5 knots. 2,679 passengers in peacetime (568 first class, 433 second class, 452 third class, 1,226 steerage).]

AGAMEMNON
(*KAISER WILHELM II*; *bottom*).
Three German four-stackers did yeoman troop work under U.S. colors in 1917–18, ferrying servicemen across the Atlantic to defeat the nation that had created them. Then, after the Armistice, they were out of work and laid up. Each had been hard-worked, particularly during the war years, and in age, all were in the 20-year range. Of the various proposals that came forth, most involved converting them for further European passenger service under American ownership. There was even talk of converting them to revolutionary diesel-driven liners. But none of the schemes came to pass. The *Von Steuben,* the former *Kronprinz Wilhelm,* was scrapped at Baltimore in 1923. The *Agamemnon,* formerly *Kaiser Wilhelm II* (seen here), and the *Mount Vernon,* the former *Kronprinzessin Cecilie,* were laid up in the backwaters of the Chesapeake. They would never see a day's work again. Their limbo lasted until 1940, when Germany was again at war. They were then both offered to the British for use as troopers but in view of their extreme age and the high cost of updating them, they were declined. Both former liners were then towed to Baltimore and junked.

PEACE AGAIN: THE TWENTIES

The First World War had changed the passenger-ship business. First of all, the great cast of characters, the liners themselves, had been shuffled. For example, among the giants, the *Lusitania* and *Britannic* gone, Germany's *Imperator* and *Bismarck* went to the British, becoming the *Berengaria* and *Majestic*. The Americans ran a superliner of their own, the first ever under Yankee colors. She too was an ex-German, the former *Vaterland*, which was rechristened as the *Leviathan*. For some other ships, the changes were less noticeable. The *George Washington* of 1908 kept her name but switched from German to American ownership. The *Amerika* followed as well, but the spelling was appropriately altered to *America*.

The North Atlantic passenger trade was different as well because of the American immigration quotas of 1921. That endless, steady and most profitable flow of immigrants was all but gone. If 1.2 million had made the westward journey in 1907, there were only a scant 150,000 in 1924. Conse-quently, most passenger-ship owners removed the old steerage spaces and replaced them with more comfortable third-class quarters. A new middle-class American tourist market had emerged and steamer firms were anxious to have a share. Of course, first-class accommodations were as well patronized as before the war. On most principal sailings, there could be found on board at least one recognizable tycoon, a silent-film starlet and any assortment of minor nobility, from exiled Russian dukes to French counts.

In addition to the customary British activity and the slowly reviving Germans, a number of other European countries emerged to claim their portion of the trade. The French produced their largest liner yet, the superb *Paris*, in 1921; Italy added its first 20,000-tonners by 1923; and two years later the Swedes commissioned their new flagship, the Atlantic's first motorliner.

AQUITANIA (above).

Just as before the War, the Cunard Line remained the most distinguished liner firm on the North Atlantic. To the envy of their competitors, both British and Continental, it had a blend of fine service, timetable schedules and a superb fleet of ships that created a large, loyal following.

On the express run between Southampton and New York, with a weekly sailing in each direction, Cunard had the distinguished "Big Three"—a trio of the world's mightiest and most luxurious liners. The *Berengaria* was the largest and therefore considered the flagship, despite her German birth; the *Aquitania* was considered the most beautiful; and the *Mauretania* continued as the world's fastest liner.

The *Aquitania* was the epitome of the great ocean liner. She was large (over four city blocks long), superbly designed and finely decorated. To the credit and pleasure of her builders, designers and owners, she was always one of the most profitable liners on the transatlantic trade.

BERENGARIA (IMPERATOR; opposite).

The flagship of Cunard during the twenties was, in fact, a German-built liner, the former *Imperator*. After the war, she was used briefly by the Americans as a troopship and was then transferred to the British government as a reparation for the *Lusitania*. The original German innards were modified, signage changed to En-

glish and, as the liner was assigned to the ownership of Cunard, the three large funnels were repainted in orange-red and black. However, there was one problem inherited from German days that remained—stability. To the very end of her days, she was known as a "tender ship."

Renamed the *Berengaria*, she had the size, power, luxury and therefore the prestige to attract a world-famous clientele. In 1924, she carried the Prince of Wales (later King Edward VIII and still later the Duke of Windsor) to New York. Traveling in first class as Lord Renfrew, the Prince's attempt at disguise fooled no one. Instead, he became a most popular passenger as he engaged in brisk walks about the upper decks, participated in the ship's tug-of-war competition and danced well into the night in the liner's ballroom (*opposite, bottom*, seen from the palm court).

Each sailing had its list of celebrities: Will Rogers, Mary Pickford and Douglas Fairbanks, Henry Ford, J. P. Morgan, the Queen of Rumania and any number of DuPonts, Astors and Vanderbilts. While fares in third class ranged between $50 and $80, a top suite in first class could cost as much as $4,000. Better rooms were often reserved for loyal passengers, but occasionally there were some slight problems. When Commodore Vanderbilt found his favorite suite on his favorite ship taken by someone else, he promptly booked it for himself for the next ten years.

MAJESTIC (BISMARCK).

Cunard's chief competitor was the White Star Line, whose ships were under the British flag but which was still owned by J. P. Morgan interests in America. It finally reverted back to full British ownership in 1926. However, White Star, still a popular company, never quite regained its sparkle of success after the First World War.

The loss of the *Titanic* remained a lingering dark cloud; the third member of their Belfast-built trio, the *Britannic*, had sunk without ever crossing the Atlantic. By the early twenties, White Star was left with an eclectic group of three large liners for its express run between Southampton and New York. The *Majestic (above)*, the incomplete German *Bismarck*, was handed over to the British and then to White Star as reparations. When she first appeared under the Union Jack, in 1922, she became the company flagship and the largest liner afloat, a prized distinction held until the appearance of 79,000-ton French *Normandie* in 1935. The views of her first-class lounge *(opposite, top)* and dining room *(opposite, bottom)* give an idea of the luxury that made her popular. Her White Star running-mates were the 46,300-ton *Olympic* and the 34,300-ton *Homeric*, another ex-German that came to the company as reparations.

OLYMPIC *(above).*

There was enormous public interest in the great liners during the twenties. Generally, they were regarded as "the largest moving objects made by man." Endless magazine and newspaper pages were filled with descriptions of their size, machinery and especially their grandeur and luxury. Local newspapers included listings of their arrival times and departures, and special columns, often with photographs, of celebrated passengers. Fashion magazines used the vast open decks as settings for some of the latest creations.

Naturally, the largest liners aroused the greatest curiosity. When one of the world's giant ships, such as the *Olympic*, shown here, went into the world's biggest drydock at Southampton, it made news. Special train excursions were organized from London, day trips that were often highlighted by walking tours around the dock itself. In the mid-twenties, for just under eight shillings, these train and inspection excursions made very popular outings.

HOMERIC *(opposite).*

The third ship of White Star's "Big Three" was the *Homeric*, a liner under construction for North German Lloyd at the time of the First War, which was ceded to the British as reparations following the Armistice. Although somewhat smaller than the *Majestic* and *Olympic*, the *Homeric* was an Atlantic liner noted for the beauty of her accommodations and her near-amazing stability at sea, a feature that won her many additional passengers.

The departures of the great liners were events in themselves. Here the *Homeric* pulls away from Manhattan's Chelsea Piers, at the foot of West 20th Street. Noted ship historian and author Frank O. Braynard once wrote:

> Sailing days were rich moments. Midnight sailings were the most glamorous, with huge liners like the *Majestic, Berengaria* and *Leviathan* attracting as many as 10,000 people to watch them depart. Hordes of visitors would come aboard and tramp through the long corridors "oh-ing" and "ah-ing" at the sumptuous lounges, the gorgeous paintings, the beautiful furniture everywhere and that special smell of wax and polish.
>
> Bon voyage packets and huge baskets of flowers would be piled up everywhere. It would take days for the stewards and others pressed into service to help get them all sorted out and delivered to the right cabins. Traffic jammed the streets near a departing liner. On one occasion, 46 people missed a sailing of the *Leviathan* because they simply could not get to Pier 86. Then, there were always a few well-wishers, who, no matter how loudly the bellboys went through the alleys clinging gongs and shouting "all ashore that's going ashore," had too good a time at the good-bye parties and forgot to get off. These sad characters would be taken off by the undocking tugs.

[Built by the Schichau Shipyards, Danzig, Germany, 1913–22. 34,351 gross tons; 774 feet long; 82 feet wide; 36-foot draft. Steam triple-expansion engines geared to twin screw. Service speed 19 knots. 2,766 passengers (529 first class, 487 second class, 1,750 third class).]

LEVIATHAN (VATERLAND; above).

Despite its position as the western end of the great transatlantic liner services, America never quite took a serious interest in the passenger-ship business. At best, the Stars and Stripes flew on a handful of smaller passenger ships. Instead, the liners of great size and highest luxury flew the colors of Britain predominantly, of France to some extent and of Germany in the years before the war. Then, after the Armistice, the ex-German *Vaterland*, the second-largest liner afloat, was in American hands. After some important military troop voyages, she was laid up until a decision could be reached on her future.

In the end, it was decided to make her the flagship of the American Merchant Marine and, as her publicity suggested, "the world's greatest ship." In reality, she was still second largest, being surpassed by White Star's *Majestic*, and not quite the fastest, the Blue Ribband still held by Cunard's *Mauretania*. But as the American flagship, she had a certain Yankee cachet. Renamed *Leviathan* in reference to her enormous proportions, part of her popularity stemmed from the new era of American tourists, who wanted to cross in a national ship. The night club (shown here) was done in particularly modern styling for the early twenties.

Unfortunately, the *Leviathan* never quite succeeded. Following her maiden trip in July 1923, she was seen as something of a "loner," since there was no other American liner of comparable size or speed that was compatible with her sailing schedule. This created schedule gaps for passengers, who often turned as an alternative to foreign-flag liners. Another problem was Prohibition. *Leviathan* spent much of her life as a "dry ship," a pressing problem for thirsty Americans. Furthermore, it was said that the service on board never quite matched that on the British and Continental liners. In the end, the *Leviathan*—while always a newsworthy and well-known liner—was one of the least successful of the giant Atlantic queens of the twenties. [Built by Blohm & Voss Shipbuilders, Hamburg, Germany, 1914. 59,956 gross tons (48,932 by British measurements); 950 feet long; 100 feet wide; 38-foot draft. Steam turbines geared to quadruple screw. Service speed 23 knots. 3,008 passengers (940 first class, 666 tourist class, 1,402 third class).]

SOUTHAMPTON OCEAN DOCKS
(opposite and overleaf).

A meeting of the world's largest ships at Southampton in the early twenties is shown at top. White Star's *Homeric* is to the left with the four-funnel *Olympic* about to depart in the background. The *Berengaria* of Cunard is to the right of center, adjacent to the *Aquitania*, another four-stacker. A small Union-Castle liner, with twin stove-pipe funnels, is at the far right.

In a dramatic aerial view *(bottom)*, the *Aquitania* is in the background, partially obscured by her own steam, and is resting in dry dock for overhaul. The *Homeric* and the four-stacker *Olympic* are berthed adjacent to one another. In the lower right corner is Royal Mail Lines' *Araguaya*.

The photograph of the docks on the following spread was taken in 1923 from the *Leviathan*. The *Olympic* is directly ahead; the *Aquitania* is to the left.

PARIS.
If the British had some of the world's largest and best-served liners, and America had the second largest, while the Germans were beginning slowly to rebuild, the French Line of the twenties had ships that were matched by great style and personality. They emphasized the element of superior service—an important consideration among passengers in the selection of a ship. Some company personnel remained with the same ship for years: some travelers looked forward to seeing the same waiter or cabin steward or purser year after year, crossing after crossing. Other personnel, the more ambitious and usually the most exacting, moved from ship to ship, generally to the company's newest liners.

Although none were among the world's largest, the French liners of the twenties were among the best decorated, possibly the most modern of their day. When, in 1912, the company introduced the four-funnel *France*, her success prompted a program for four more liners, all built separately—not as sisters—in an evolutionary progression. Consequently, the new French liners not only grew in size but represented the finest in new decorative stylings. The three-funnel *Paris*, intended for completion in 1916

but delayed by the war until 1921, was something of a magical ship in the twenties. Her innards were splendid Art Nouveau but with hints of what was to become Art Deco. She featured some of the best food on the Atlantic and had an on-board ambience and personality that, especially to Americans, gave the most glittering impressions of Parisian life. A French Line advertising slogan enhanced this concept: "France, you know, really starts at Pier 57, New York!"

Along with their superb kitchens and overall shipboard ambience and style, the French liners were noted for their extravagant suites and deluxe apartments in first class. Such rooms, generally named for a national region or city rather than being numbered, were often decorated in a variety of styles and decors. The rooms usually had windows rather than portholes, separate bedrooms *(above)* and one or more full bathrooms, and possibly a sitting or drawing room, trunk room, dressing room, entrance foyer and even an adjoining servant's cabin. Here a phone is placed between the twin beds. Such a convenience was an extreme rarity aboard liners, no matter how large, in the early twenties. Passenger liners were done in every possible style and period: Egyptian, Italian Renaissance, Moorish, Spanish, Louis XIV, XV and XVI, Empire, Georgian, Queen Anne, Jacobean, Tudor, Art Nouveau, Art Deco and even Bauhaus.

The ultimate in first-class travel in the twenties was to cross the Atlantic, preferably in a well-known, large liner, along with one's own touring car *(right)*. Some passengers took personal servants, pets, magnificent jewels and that classic standard of ocean travel, the steamer trunk. [Built by Chantiers de l'Atlantique, St. Nazaire, France, 1921. 34,569 gross tons; 764 feet long; 85 feet wide. Steam turbines geared to quadruple screw. Service speed 22 knots. 1,930 passengers (560 first class, 530 second class, 840 third class).].

DEUTSCHLAND (1924) **and** **ALBERT BALLIN.**
The Hamburg-America Line was equally depleted, devastated
and stripped after the war. Rebuilding was slow. The company
policy of building large and luxurious liners was abandoned in
favor of more moderate ships that offered exceptionally comfortable accommodations. The first new passenger ships even hinted
at the past, using the four masts reminiscent of many turn-of-the-
century liners and also of the nineteenth-century sailships. With
the great age of immigration past, Hamburg-America built their
first new Atlantic liners, sister ships known as the *Albert Ballin*
and *Deutschland (above)*, with a balanced capacity for 1,558 passengers and six large cargo holds. These ships, trading between
Hamburg and New York in ten days in each direction, with stop-
overs at Southampton and Cherbourg on the way, earned their
profits from both the passenger and the freight business.

The sister ships offered very fine first-class accommodations,
in accordance with the high prewar standards of Hamburg-America. The first-class section occupied six decks and included a large
sports deck and open-air bowling alley. The dining services included a special grill room, with an à la carte menu and a special
entrance fee. The public areas included a glass-enclosed promenade, a smoking room *(opposite, top;* on the *Albert Ballin)*, writing room, library, ladies' parlor, social hall and terrace café. There
was also a children's dining room, indoor tiled pool, gymnasium,
elevator, gift shop and florist.

The terrace café on the *Albert Ballin (opposite, bottom)* was a
modified, smaller version of the prewar winter garden. The purpose was similar: to remind passengers of shoreside comfort and
delight, with live greenery to hint at country life. Facing aft to the
stern, great flaps could be opened that filled the area with full
daylight and a gentle sea breeze. [*Deutschland* and *Albert Ballin*:
built by Blohm & Voss Shipbuilders, Hamburg, Germany, 1924.
20,607 gross tons; 627 feet long; 72 feet wide. Steam turbines
geared to twin screw. Service speed 15.5 knots. 1,558 passengers
(221 first class, 402 second class, 935 third class).]

COLUMBUS (above).

The North German Lloyd had just started construction of two new 35,000-tonners when the First World War erupted. Progress halted and the ships sat out the war years as mere steel shells. The new sister ships, the *Columbus* and *Hindenburg*, had been envisioned as the flagships for the Lloyd on the Atlantic. Then, after the Armistice, the *Columbus* was given to the British, becoming the White Star Line's *Homeric*. However, the second ship remained with the Germans. Work progressed at a sluggish pace because of shortages and ever-increasing costs. Abandoning her intended name, she was christened the *Columbus* and crossed to New York for the first time in April 1924, signaling the slow recovery of the once-mighty North German Lloyd liner fleet. [Built by the Schichau Shipyards, Danzig, Germany, 1924. 32,581 gross tons; 775 feet long; 83 feet wide; 36-foot draft. Steam turbines geared to twin screw. Service speed 23 knots. 1,725 passengers (479 cabin class, 644 tourist class, 602 third class).]

RELIANCE (opposite, top).

Recovery for the German liner companies was often a difficult process. Two intended 20,000-tonners, the *William O'Swald* and the *Johann Heinrich Burchard*, were still under construction for Hamburg-America when the war broke out in 1914. Then, like so many other German passenger ships, they became reparations at war's end, both going to the Royal Holland Lloyd of Amsterdam. The *O'Swald* became the *Brabantia* while the *Burchard* changed to the *Limburgia*. For two years, the pair traded between Holland and the east coast of South America. Then, in 1922, they were sold to the United American Lines of New York and became the *Resolute* and *Reliance* (shown here), respectively, for the transatlantic trade between Hamburg and New York. Operations were in conjunction with the Hamburg-America Line, the original owners of the two ships. Then, in 1926, through a variety of complications, both ships were sold to Hamburg-America. After more than ten years (but keeping their American-selected names), the twin liners were finally back with their intended owners. Thereafter the *Resolute* and *Reliance* developed very fine reputations, particularly as cruise ships. [*Reliance*: J. C. Tecklenborg Shipyard, Geestemünde, Germany, 1920. 19,582 gross tons; 615 feet long; 71 feet wide. Triple expansion engines and one steam turbine geared to triple screw. Service speed 16 knots. 1,010 passengers (290 first class, 320 second class, 400 third class).]

CLEVELAND (opposite, bottom).

Another German liner that endured an ever-changing career before rejoining the postwar Hamburg-America Line was the *Cleveland*. Built in 1909 in the classic four-masted design of the period, she was used on the Hamburg run, both to New York and Boston. She spent the war years idle at her German homeport and was allocated to the U.S. Government as reparations in 1919. Converted to a troop transport, she became the U.S.S. *Mobile*. A year later she was chartered to the hard-pressed White Star Line for a series of immigrant trips between Liverpool and New York. Later in that year she was sold to the Byron Steamship Company of London, becoming the *King Alexander* for immigrant service between the Greek port of Piraeus and New York. In 1923, she went back to the Americans, joining the United American Lines and reverting to her original name, the *Cleveland*. Shortly thereafter, as she returned to the Hamburg–New York route, her sailings were coordinated with her original German owners. In 1926, the Hamburg-America Line repurchased their former ship. [Built by Blohm & Voss Shipbuilders, Hamburg, Germany, 1909. 16,971 gross tons; 607 feet long; 63 feet wide. Steam quadruple expansion engines geared to twin screw. Service speed 15.5 knots. 1,600 passengers (600 cabin class, 1,000 third class).]

ALBERTIC *(above).*

The greatest and grandest Atlantic steamship firms ran, in addition to their more notable flagships and record-breakers, whole fleets of lesser-known intermediate ships, often referred to as "cabin liners." Not only did these ships trade on the lucrative New York run, but also crossed to ports such as Boston, Philadelphia, Quebec City, Montreal and those of the Canadian Maritime Provinces.

Some of these passenger ships changed hands frequently. White Star's *Albertic* had been designed and laid down as North German Lloyd's *München*. The war halted construction. At the end of the conflict, she was handed over to Britain's Royal Mail Lines and became the *Ohio*. She joined White Star in 1927 and served with them until the Depression, when she was broken up in Japan. [Built by Weser Shipbuilders, Bremen, Germany, 1914–23. 18,940 gross tons; 615 feet long; 71 feet wide. Quadruple expansion engines geared to twin screw. Service speed 17 knots. 1,442 passengers (229 first class, 523 second class, 690 third class).]

MONTCALM *(opposite, top).*

Sister ships such as the *Montcalm*, *Montrose* and *Montclare* were Canadian Pacific's intermediate liners on the Atlantic trade to eastern Canada. Sailing out of Liverpool, the ships went along the St. Lawrence to Quebec City and Montreal in the ice-free months between April and December. In deep winter, they terminated their crossings at St. John, New Brunswick. [Built by John Brown & Company Limited, Clydebank, Scotland, 1921. 16,418 gross tons; 575 feet long; 70 feet wide. Steam turbines geared to twin screw. Service speed 16 knots. 1,810 passengers (542 cabin class, 1,268 third class).]

LACONIA *(opposite, bottom).*

The great Cunard Company built a near assembly line of intermediate-type passenger liners. They were all given a balanced profile of two tall masts and a single, rather slender stack. Their passenger accommodations left sizable spaces for freight. The *Laconia*, the third in a series of over a dozen similar ships, could take 2,180 passengers at full capacity as well as six holds of cargo. [Built by Swan, Hunter & Wigham Richardson Limited, Newcastle-upon-Tyne, England, 1921. 19,680 gross tons; 623 feet long; 73 feet wide. Steam turbines geared to twin screw. Service speed 16 knots. 2,180 passengers (340 first class, 340 second class, 1,500 third class).]

TRANSYLVANIA (above).

Britain's Anchor Line built a series of five similar sister ships between 1920 and 1925 specifically for the immigrant trade to the United States from Scotland and Ireland. The first three liners—the *Cameronia, Tuscania* and *California*—were sturdy but rather plain-looking with their single stacks. They were not as popular as the company had hoped. For the final pair of sisters, the designers decided on three stacks. This final pair was notably more successful, especially with the immigrant trade, who still believed that "the more stacks, the more secure and safer the ship." The *Transylvania* (shown here) and her twin sister, the *Caledonia*, were two of the most popular liners on the North Atlantic run in the twenties. [Built by Fairfield Shipbuilding & Engineering Company, Glasgow, Scotland, 1925. 16,923 gross tons; 552 feet long; 70 feet wide. Steam turbines geared to twin screw. Service speed 16 knots. 1,423 passengers (279 first class, 344 second class, 800 third class).]

VEENDAM and VOLENDAM (opposite).

Following the war, the Holland-America Line—among others—realized that, because of quotas imposed by the American Immi-gration Act of 1921, the age of a booming steerage market was over. Consequently, for their first new postwar passenger ships, the company built two medium-sized vessels of a mere 15,400 tons each. Known as the *Veendam* and *Volendam*, the two sisters settled down to a practical life: summers on the North Atlantic trading between Rotterdam, the Channel ports and New York and then winters on cruises from New York, either to the Caribbean or farther afield to the Mediterranean. A photograph taken when the *Veendam* was outbound from New York *(opposite, top)*, also shows the American passenger ship *Orizaba* (left) and the tanker *Franklin* (right).

The library aboard the *Volendam (opposite, bottom)* reflected Dutch decor of the period. The atmosphere was cozy, an arrangement of wholesome comfort. High-gloss mahogany paneling was offset by groups of soft armchairs and sofas on a matching carpet. [*Veendam*: Built by Harland & Wolff Limited, Govan, Scotland, 1923. 15,450 gross tons; 579 feet long; 67 feet wide. Steam turbines geared to twin screw. Service speed 15 knots. 1,898 passengers (262 first class, 436 second class, 1,200 third class).]

ROMA (opposite, top).

In 1926–27, Italy added its two largest liners yet, the first pair that could seriously compete with the better-known north European ships. The first of the pair, the *Roma*, was commissioned in September 1926. She established an express sailing pattern: from Naples and then Genoa, a call at Villefranche on the French Riviera and then at Gibraltar (for Spanish passengers) and finally across to New York. A year or so later, she was joined by a sister ship, the *Augustus*. The only apparent differences between this set was that the *Roma* was given steam turbines while the *Augustus* was fitted with diesels, making her more distinctive. She was the largest motorliner ever built. [*Roma*: Built by Ansaldo Shipyards, Genoa, Italy, 1926. 32,583 gross tons; 709 feet long; 82 feet wide. Steam turbines geared to quadruple screw. Service speed 22 knots. 1,675 passengers (375 first class, 600 second class, 700 third class).]

COLOMBO (opposite, bottom).

Unlike many of the north European steamer firms in the twenties, the Italian companies were still supported by a vast flow of immigrants seeking passage to North America. Consequently, a series of smaller, less fancy ships were employed, with large capacities in either third class or steerage, primarily on the mainline run between Naples, Genoa and New York. The steamer *Colombo*, her outer decks crowded with immigrants, is seen docking at New York's Pier 96, at the foot of West 56th Street. Many immigrant passengers settled within blocks of the pier, in the tenements of New York's West Side. Others remained within a five-

mile radius of the very dock where they first landed. [Built by Palmers Shipbuilding & Iron Company Limited, Jarrow-on-Tyne, England, 1915–21. 11,762 gross tons; 536 feet long; 64 feet wide. Steam quadruple expansion engines geared to twin screw. Service speed 16 knots. 2,800 passengers (100 first class, 700 third class, 2,000 steerage).]

BERGENSFJORD (above).

The passenger ships of the Norwegian-America Line, a firm formed in 1910 to represent Norway on the North Atlantic, was unique in using piers in the Bay Ridge section of Brooklyn, about five miles south of the customary liner berths of Manhattan. Liners such as the *Bergensfjord* landed thousands of Norwegian immigrants and it is especially interesting to note that a large Scandinavian community, composed mostly of Norwegians, reside to this day in an area just blocks away from the same Brooklyn pier. The *Bergensfjord*—along with her fleet mate, the *Stavangerfjord*—worked a monthly service from Oslo, Kristiansand, Stavanger, Bergen and Copenhagen and then across to Halifax (to land Canada-bound immigrants) and finally the turnaround at Brooklyn. [Built by Cammell, Laird & Company Limited, Birkenhead, England, 1913. 10,666 gross tons; 530 feet long; 61 feet wide. Steam quadruple expansion engines geared to twin screw. Service speed 15 knots. 1,081 passengers (105 first class, 216 second class, 760 third class).]

GRIPSHOLM (above).

When the Swedish-American Line decided to build their first brand-new liner, for the North Atlantic run between Gothenburg, Copenhagen and New York, the management opted for a novel, distinctive ship. Instead of the traditional steam-turbine drive, she was fitted with diesel engines. In doing so, the new *Gripsholm* was the first motorliner on the Atlantic run. [Built by Armstrong, Whitworth & Company Limited, Newcastle-upon-Tyne, England, 1925. 17,993 gross tons; 573 feet long; 74 feet wide. Burmeister & Wain diesels geared to twin screw. Service speed 16 knots. 1,557 passengers (127 first class, 482 second class, 948 third class).]

DROTTNINGHOLM (opposite).

Many passengers formed great attachments to the liners. These loyalties remained for years in the form of vivid memories. Here are the recollections of Richard Sandstrom, an American of Swedish ancestry who made a number of passages to the land of his heritage:

> In 1930, my father crossed on the *Drottningholm* [opposite, top]. He had become quite friendly with some of the staff members and they began to visit our home in New Jersey. In those days, the Swedish liners arrived on Monday or Tuesday and remained in New York until a Saturday morning sailing. There was always enough time for visits by the crew.
>
> Later, I crossed on the *Drottningholm* myself and, since I had al-
> ready met a good number of the staff, there was an enormous sense of familiarity for me. The ship was akin to an old seashore hotel where little seemed to change. I especially loved the old smoking room, which admitted only men in those days. It had the atmosphere of a mellow country inn.
>
> I remember the *Drottningholm* as a great roller at sea. She was also one of the first Atlantic liners to have an enclosed promenade deck, which was always a very popular social spot for meeting fellow passengers. We ordered our bath at a specific hour (only four cabins on the entire ship had private facilities). This was arranged with the cabin steward, who in turn notified the bathroom steward. Of course, passengers didn't bathe every day, at least on northern Atlantic crossings.
>
> Our cabin-class stateroom (cabin class onboard the *Drottningholm* was the equivalent to first class in many other passenger ships of the day) did not have a chest of drawers. Instead, for the ten-day crossing, almost all passengers traveled with a wardrobe trunk. These were placed in the baggage room and could be visited at specific times. I can't quite remember what we did with soiled laundry. It was an age long before drip-dry!

The cabin-class dining room on board the *Drottningholm (opposite, bottom)* included a skylight in the center and a fireplace. [Built by Alexander Stephen & Sons Limited, Glasgow, Scotland, 1905. 11,182 gross tons; 538 feet long; 60 feet wide. Steam turbines geared to triple screw. Service speed 17 knots. 1,386 passengers (532 cabin class, 854 third class).]

BELGENLAND (above).

During the twenties, the transatlantic passenger trade slackened somewhat, especially as the vast numbers of immigrants in steerage had diminished. Consequently, many steamer firms turned toward cruising as an alternative. These luxury voyages became increasingly more popular, particularly the more extensive trips which catered to the likes of American tycoons, Hollywood aristocrats and exiled European royalty. Zita, the last empress of Austria, was a favorite passenger on board many of the world cruiseships.

Red Star Line's *Belgenland* was among the most popular cruise liners in the twenties. She was particularly noted for her sailings around the world, as exemplified by a departure from New York on December 4, 1924. There was a 133-day itinerary that touched at 60 ports in 14 countries for a total of 28,130 miles. Her port calls were lengthy, useful for overland excursions, and included such highlights as 17 days ashore in Japan, China and Korea; 18 days in India; and 8 days in Egypt and the Holy Land. [Built by Harland & Wolff Limited, Belfast, Northern Ireland, 1914–17. 24,578 gross tons; 697 feet long; 78 feet wide. Steam triple expansion turbines geared to triple screw. Service speed 17 knots. 2,600 passengers (500 first class, 600 second class, 1,500 third class).]

RELIANCE (opposite).

Hamburg-America's sister ships *Reliance* and *Resolute*, known as the "white cruising yachts," were great favorites during the twenties. Their voyages were quite diverse. In the winter of 1926, for example, the *Reliance* made a series of all-first-class runs to the Caribbean islands: 27 days for a minimum fare of $250 and 14 days for $150. The *Resolute* left New York for a four-month cruise around the world. For this trip, fares began at $1,500, a price that also included all shore excursions.

CARINTHIA (above).

The Cunarders ran a particularly diverse program of cruises that included Mediterranean trips in the illustrious *Mauretania*. Other voyages were made in some of the company's medium-sized ships. The *Scythia* sailed from New York in January 1926 for a 66-day tour of the Mediterranean. Minimum fares began at $925 and, once again, included all shore excursions. In April, the *Carinthia*, seen here, followed suit and set sail for a 41-day jaunt to the Mediterranean lands. Her fares started at $625. On both liners, passenger accommodations were made all first class and exclusive; the *Scythia's* capacity was cut drastically from 2,206 to a mere 385 while the *Carinthia* was reduced from 1,650 to 400. [*Carinthia*: Built by Vickers Armstrong Shipbuilders Limited, Barrow-in-Furness, England, 1925. 20,277 gross tons; 624 feet long; 73 feet wide. Steam turbines geared to twin screw. Service speed 16 knots. 1,650 passengers (240 first class, 460 second class, 950 third class).]

ALGONQUIN (opposite, top).

In an age long before the invasion of aircraft, roundtrip cruise voyages were offered frequently between two American ports. For example, the American-flag Clyde-Mallory Lines used passenger steamers such as the *Algonquin* in regular service between New York and Galveston with a call at Miami in each direction. [Built by Newport News Shipbuilding & Drydock Company, Newport News, Virginia, 1925. 5,950 gross tons; 402 feet long; 55 feet wide. Steam turbines geared to single screw. Service speed 16 knots. 300 one-class passengers.]

SHAWNEE (opposite, bottom).

Other Clyde-Mallory liners, such as the *Shawnee* (shown here) and her sister ship *Iroquois*, offered regularly scheduled runs between New York, Charleston and Jacksonville. Such a trade appealed to many. The ships departed from Jacksonville on Friday evenings, then made a Saturday morning call at Charleston and finally arrived at New York on Monday morning. The "long weekend" at sea could cost as little as $37.50.

Of course, ships such as the *Shawnee* were not solely dependent upon passengers but also carried considerable cargo as well. Among other items, the *Shawnee* often steamed into New York harbor loaded with thousands of crates of Florida oranges. [Built by Newport News Shipbuilding & Drydock Company, 1927. 6,200 gross tons; 409 feet long; 62 feet wide; 21-foot draft. Steam turbines geared to twin screw. Service speed 18 knots. 600 one-class passengers.]

AMERICA (AMERIKA).

Passenger ships suffered any number of fates and calamities: collisions, sinkings, fires, groundings, capsizings and, on occasion, mysterious disappearances without trace. The *America* of the United States Lines was being refitted at the Newport News Shipyard in Virginia on March 10, 1926, when fire broke out. It spread rapidly but the vessel was saved. Completed as the German *Amerika* in 1905, her career spanned 53 years in which she rammed and sank two ships, was sunk herself and was nearly gutted by fire. Furthermore, she sailed as a passenger liner for three different owners and served as a troopship in two world wars.

SHIPS OF EMPIRE

During the twenties, passenger ships still provided the best global links. Sensibly, shipowners created appropriate fleets that supported the vast political, economic and social ties that existed. Such ships carried passengers, often in several classes, as well as below-deck cargos, the general goods out of the homelands and then the returning colonial freights.

Passenger ships provided the connections for the colonial empires—the Dutch with their East Indies, the French with Indochina and the British, who still commanded the biggest colonial network on earth. The decks and lounges of such ships reflected their work, with passenger lists that included colonial officials, government administrators and their entourages, civil servants, troops, teachers, police, doctors, nurses, scientists, missionaries and the perpetual traders. Steamers on one of the Indian Ocean runs would have lounges complete with bamboo furnishings, potted palms and overhead fans, and might carry plantation owners bound for Java, tea planters to and from Ceylon and spice merchants of India.

Not all of the ships included in this section were part of a political system. Some ships were assigned to highly lucrative trades, such as that between Italy and South America or between Germany and Argentina, which represented social as well as economic bonds. Third-class immigrants were often a substantial part of such operations.

Of course, most of these ships were just as important for their cargo services. In addition to regular passengers and tourists, the *Bermuda* carried fresh water from New York to the island of the same name. The Blue Funnel ships delivered steel for a new bridge in Burma, the P&O liners unloaded railway equipment at Bombay and the Royal Mail vessels carried British-made machinery to Brazil. Until the political links changed, these ships on their global trade were assured of a steady flow of both passengers and cargo.

BERMUDA *(opposite)*.

The British islands of Bermuda were a natural for a passenger-ship service. They were a mere 600 miles from New York, a sea journey of some 40 hours. The Furness Withy Company of London began such an operation with a series of small, second-hand passenger ships. In quick time, the vacation attributes of Bermuda became apparent to many Americans. Consequently, Furness ordered a large, brand-new cruiseship for the run. She was completed in 1927 as the *Bermuda (opposite, top)*. Round-trip six-day cruises were offered for $50.

The ship offered a number of deluxe suites in her first-class accommodations *(opposite, bottom)*. Such quarters often featured a bedroom, sitting room, entrance foyer and private bathroom.

The *Bermuda* was one of the most unfortunate passenger ships of all time. Just over three years after her completion, in June 1931, she was seriously damaged by fire at her pier in Hamilton, Bermuda. However, her owners felt that repairs were economically feasible. She crossed to her builders' yard at Belfast only to have a second, even more tragic fire erupt in November. She was finished. Almost all of her upper decks burned out and she sank at her pier. But there were still more problems. After being salvaged for scrap, she was under tow in May 1932, bound for Rosyth in

Scotland, when she went aground. Few ships have had such a sad demise. [Built by Workman, Clark & Company Limited, Belfast, Northern Ireland, 1927. 19,086 gross tons; 547 feet long; 74 feet wide. Doxford diesels geared to quadruple screw. Service speed 17 knots. 691 passengers (616 first class, 75 second class).]

LAFAYETTE *(above)*.

Like most major European powers, the French maintained a fleet of passenger ships, with limited cargo capacities, especially for mail, to service the overseas outposts. The French Line, which was Government-owned, had a special fleet of vessels that traded to the Caribbean islands of Guadeloupe and Martinique and to French Guiana. The *Lafayette*—which had spent some years on the New York run out of Le Havre—was, in the later years of her career, placed on the colonial West Indies trade. [Built by Chantiers et Ateliers de Provence, Port du Bouc, France, 1915. 12,220 gross tons; 563 feet long; 64 feet wide. Steam triple expansion engines geared to quadruple screw. Service speed 18 knots. 1,250 passengers (336 first class, 110 second class, 90 third class, 714 steerage).]

CARTAGO (opposite, top).

With its great banana plantations, the United Fruit Company had a corporate empire in the Caribbean and Central America. To assist with this operation and the transport of goods, general cargo southbound and as many as 200,000 bunches of bananas per trip northward, the firm built a series of passenger-cargo ships. Ships such as the *Cartago* could carry as many as 100 first-class passengers, including company executives and plantation managers, their families, traders, scientists and, of course, the ordinary tourists. Many travelers preferred the United Fruit "banana boats" because of their more leisurely sailing patterns to exotic, more remote tropical ports. [Built by Workman, Clark & Company Limited, Belfast, Northern Ireland, 1908. 4,732 gross tons; 419 feet long; 49 feet wide. Steam triple expansion engines geared to single screw. Service speed 14 knots. 100 first-class passengers.]

CAP ARCONA (opposite, bottom).

The harsh economic conditions in Germany during the twenties prompted thousands to move elsewhere, to places such as Brazil and Argentina. The Hamburg–South America Line built a special series of vessels that suited the situation by carrying only third-class and steerage passengers. However, for the more palatial trade, the company built a grand three-stacker that was affectionately thought of as "the most wonderful ship in the German merchant navy."

The *Cap Arcona*, commissioned in November 1927, included luxurious features. Every first-class cabin was outside and included private bathroom facilities (in itself very much a rarity), a restaurant that was located on the upper promenade deck and that included 20 windows overlooking the seas below, a full gymnasium and heatable salt-water pool and a large open-air tennis court on the deck just aft of the third funnel. For several years, the *Cap Arcona* was the "queen of the South Atlantic." The Germans

were delighted. [Built by Blohm & Voss Shipbuilders, Hamburg, Germany, 1927. 27,560 gross tons; 676 feet long; 84 feet wide. Steam turbines geared to twin screw. Service speed 20 knots. 1,315 passengers (575 first class, 275 second class, 465 third class).]

ASTURIAS (above).

In the mid-twenties, Britain's Royal Mail Lines added two notable liners, the twin sisters *Asturias* (shown here) and *Alcantara*. From the beginning, both ships attracted considerable attention. Since Royal Mail placed a high priority on the greatest possible degree of cargo space (for the general cargo going southbound to Brazil and Argentina, and then for the Argentine beef returning to Britain), the designers of the pair selected diesel propulsion, then relatively new. The fitting of the diesels eliminated the space needed for a boiler room. Thus, in view of their 22,000 tons, the Royal Mail sisters were the largest and fastest motorliners in the world at the time of their completion in 1926–27 (surpassing Sweden's 17,000-ton *Gripsholm*, the previously largest motorliner, finished in 1925).

The accommodations on board were considered among the most luxurious and comfortable yet seen on the South American trade. The public rooms were fashioned after popular examples of British and Empire domestic stylings. Particularly outstanding was the two-deck high French Empire dining room, which seated 400 at a single sitting, and also the 29-foot-long indoor swimming pool, an amenity that proved itself admirably during sailings in the tropics. [Built by Harland & Wolff Limited, Belfast, Northern Ireland, 1926. 22,071 gross tons; 656 feet long; 78 feet wide. Burmeister & Wain type diesels geared to twin screw. Service speed 16 knots. 1,410 passengers (410 first class, 232 second class, 768 third class).]

ANDALUSIA STAR *(above)*.

Britain's Blue Star Line avoided the immigrant traffic that was so much a part of the South American liner trade. Instead, concentration was placed on all-first-class, deluxe passenger quarters and a large freight capacity that was linked to the meat cargos coming northward to Britain. Blue Star was owned by the Vestey Group, which in turn owned a large meat-processing and butcher-shop business in Britain.

Because of the leisurely voyages from London, via Portugal and the Canaries, and then onward to Rio de Janeiro, Santos, Montevideo and Buenos Aires, round-trip holiday-seeking passengers often selected Blue Star combination liners such as the *Andalucia Star*. There were lengthy turn-around stays in South America (caused mostly by the loading and unloading operations) that were useful for a full-cruise voyage. The on-board service tended to be exclusive, with a club-like atmosphere. Passengers often repeated the voyage year after year, requesting the same stateroom and the same cabin steward. [Built by Cammell Laird & Company Limited, 1927. 12,846 gross tons; 535 feet long; 68 feet wide. Steam turbines geared to twin screw. Service speed 16 knots. 180 first-class passengers.]

VULCANIA and SATURNIA *(opposite)*.

Italy's Cosulich Line produced two very fine motorliners that could be swung with relative ease between summers on the Atlantic run—between Trieste, Venice and New York—and winters on a more southerly course—from Italy to Brazil, Uruguay and Argentina. Consisting of the *Saturnia* and *Vulcania* (shown here), the pair ranked as the two of the largest motorliners afloat and were given the low, almost squat profiles that were generally used for diesel-driven ships at the time.

Long after most of the other European and British liner firms were turning their attention to more modern and contemporary stylings, such as the Art Deco then in vogue, the Italians persisted with period decor. The white wood panels and the gilt in the *Vulcania's* first-class ballroom suggested a prewar ambiance. [Built by Cantiere Navale Triestino, Monfalcone, Italy, 1927. 23,970 gross tons; 631 feet long; 79 feet wide. Burmeister & Wain diesels geared to twin screw. Service speed 19 knots. 2,196 passengers (279 first class, 257 second class, 310 third class, 1,350 fourth class).]

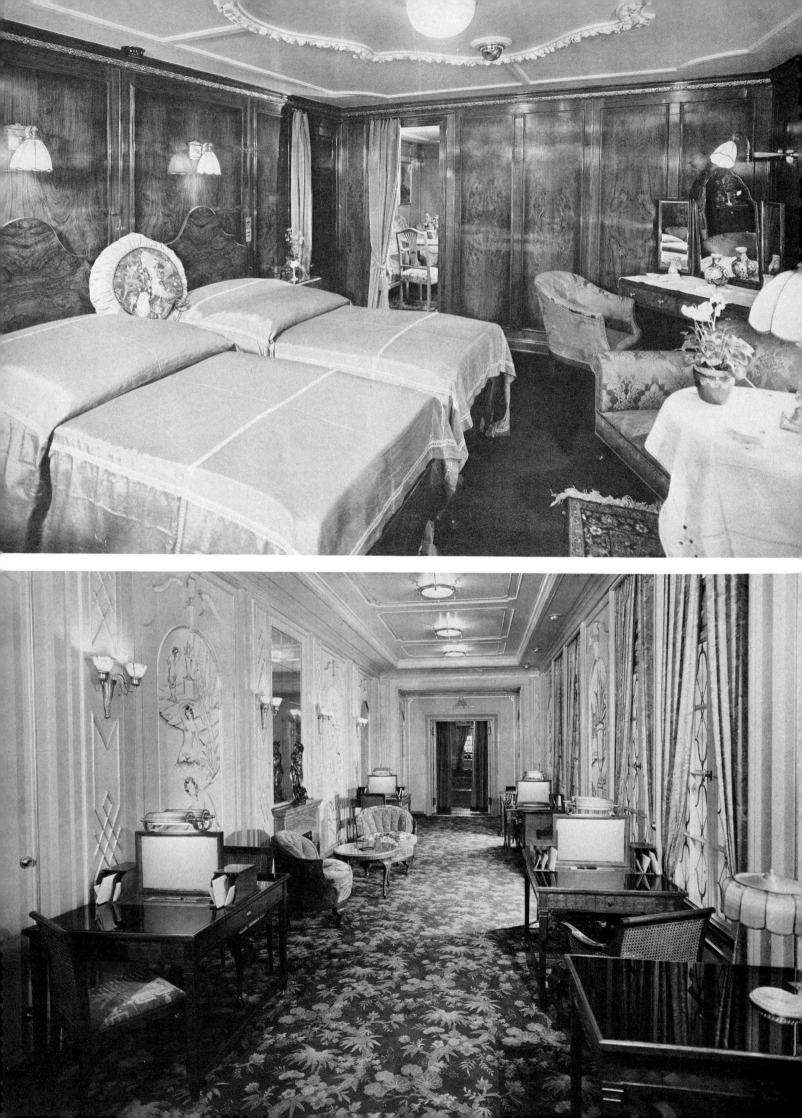

The *Vulcania* and *Saturnia*. The *Vulcania's* Imperial Suite *(opposite, top)* included a bedroom (with beds instead of bunks), a sitting area, special drawing room and private bathroom.

The first-class writing room *(opposite, bottom)* was one of her more modern shipboard public spaces.

The grand staircase in first class aboard the *Saturnia (above)*, the sistership to the *Vulcania*, featured an elaborately carved panel.

CONTE BIANCAMANO.

Another Italian liner firm, the Lloyd Sabaudo, added two fine liners in the mid-twenties, the *Conte Biancamano (opposite, top)* and *Conte Grande*. Large, sufficiently fast and with adequate passenger accommodations, these ships were, in the course of events, shifted among a variety of services that reflected Italy's political and economic ties. In the years prior to the Second World War, the *Conte Biancamano* and her sister sailed to New York, the east coast of South America, South Africa, India and then farther out to China, and even on some trooping voyages to colonial East Africa.

The smoking room aboard the *Conte Biancamano (opposite, bottom)* was done in mahogany. Two decks in height, it included a bar at one end and an ornate fireplace, complete with electric fire,

at the other. Note the electric ceiling fan in the top-left corner.

Although the ship was a medium-sized liner by world standards, and hardly the largest in the Italian fleet, she did not lack splendors. Her first-class ballroom *(above)*, sporting a ceiling with murals, rose three decks in height. The room was often used for afternoon and evening concerts. For dancing, the carpet would be rolled and removed, exposing a finely worked hardwood floor. [Built by William Beardmore & Company Limited, Glasgow, Scotland, 1925. 24,416 gross tons; 653 feet long; 76 feet wide. Steam turbines geared to twin screw. Service speed 20 knots. 1,750 passengers (280 first class, 420 second class, 390 third class, 660 fourth class).]

WINDSOR CASTLE (opposite, top).

The Union-Castle Line remained dominant in the African trades after the First World War. Just as the conflict erupted, the company was planning its largest ships to date, two liners that would be the only (and the last) four-stackers designed for a route other than the North Atlantic. The first, the *Arundel Castle*, was laid down in 1915. When construction resumed in 1918, the original pattern was rather dated. The *Arundel Castle* appeared first in April 1921. The *Windsor Castle* (seen here) having been named by the Prince of Wales (later King Edward VIII, then the Duke of Windsor), followed in April of the next year. Thereafter, for some years, the two sisters were the prime liners on Union-Castle's mail run between Southampton and the South African Cape. [*Windsor Castle*: Built by John Brown & Company Limited, Clydebank, Scotland, 1922. 18,967 gross tons; 661 feet long; 72 feet wide. Steam turbines geared to twin screw. Service speed 17 knots. 870 passengers (235 first class, 360 second class, 275 third class).]

CARNARVON CASTLE (opposite, bottom).

By the mid-twenties, Union-Castle was following a pattern set by many liner companies. They were deeply impressed with the new generation of low, squat-stack motorliners. Such ships were considered more efficient and required less engine-room space, thus releasing profitable space for passenger or cargo areas. When the *Carnarvon Castle* was first introduced in the summer of 1926, she signaled a new breed of ships, both for Union-Castle and others. [Built by Harland & Wolff Limited, Belfast, Northern Ireland, 1926. 20,063 gross tons; 656 feet long; 74 feet wide. Burmeister & Wain diesels geared to twin screw. Service speed 16 knots. 853 passengers (311 first class, 276 second class, 266 third class).]

USARAMO (above).

The German Africa Line was the mainline link for German traders, government officials and tourists to colonial and trading outposts in East, West and Southern Africa. Small passenger steamers such as the *Usaramo* made the slow but important passages from Hamburg to the Channel and then southward to West African ports before rounding the Cape and sailing northward for her calls in East Africa. [Built by Blohm & Voss Shipbuilders, Hamburg, Germany, 1920. 7,775 gross tons; 450 feet long; 56 feet wide. Steam turbine geared to single screw. Service speed 14 knots. 261 passengers (101 first class, 62 second class, 98 third class).]

RANPURA (above).

Next to Cunard, the P&O Steam Navigation Company Limited—often referred to simply as "the P&O"—was perhaps the most legendary of the British steamship firms. P&O ships followed the building and development of the British Empire—first to Egypt and the Suez, then to India and finally to Australia and the Far East. All of its passenger ships followed a similar sailing pattern: out from London, through the Mediterranean and then the Suez Canal, along the Red Sea and finally into the Indian Ocean. Because it was often a very warm-weather operation, knowledgeable passengers preferred portside cabins outbound, on the ship's shaded side, and starboard side rooms on the return. The process was given a simple abbreviation: port outward, starboard home. Some people hold that this slogan was turned into the adjective "posh," which has been used ever since to mean "very elegant."

In the twenties, P&O maintained a large fleet of express ships and auxiliary vessels. For the express run from London to Bombay via Suez, there were four sisters, all with Indian names: *Ranpura* (seen here), *Ranchi*, *Rawalpindi* and *Rajputana*. [*Ranpura*: Built by Hawthorn, Leslie & Company Limited, Newcastle, England, 1925. 16,585 gross tons; 570 feet long; 71 feet wide. Steam quadruple expansion engines geared to twin screw. Service speed 17 knots. 590 passengers (310 first class, 280 second class).]

CITY OF SIMLA (opposite, top).

Britain's Ellerman Lines was, for many years, one of the largest shipping firms in the world. Their scope was global. Although the majority of its ships were freighters, some others were fitted with first-class passenger accommodations, mostly for the trade between London and ports in India or South Africa. All of them had "city" names: *City of Canterbury, City of Durban, City of Hong Kong, City of Poona* and *City of Simla* (shown here). [Built by William Gray & Company, West Hartlepool, England, 1921. 9,468 gross tons; 476 feet long; 58 feet wide. Steam turbines geared to twin screw. Service speed 13.5 knots. Approximately 100 first-class passengers.]

TAIREA (opposite, bottom).

The British India Line not only had operations from Britain but used India itself as a base for its numerous and diverse schedules. There were runs to East and South Africa, the Persian Gulf, Southeast Asia, Australia and even northward along the Asian coast.

The three-funnel *Tairea*—and her sisters *Takliwa* and *Talamba*—appeared much larger than their mere 7,900 tons, possibly because of the number of their stacks. In their dark, stonelike coloring, the trio worked on the Indian Ocean service between Bombay and East African ports such as Zanzibar, Dar-es-Salaam, Mombasa and Durban. Colonials, traders and the privileged traveled in the comforts of first class. Others, far less fortunate, used the ships as deck passengers for short, overnight passages. [Built by Barclay, Curle & Company Limited, Glasgow, Scotland, 1924. 7,933 gross tons; 465 feet long; 60 feet wide. Steam triple expansion engines geared to twin screw. Service speed 16 knots. 130 saloon passengers and approximately 1,000 deck passengers.]

INDRAPOERA (above).

The Dutch colonial trade to the East Indies was supported by two rival firms: the Amsterdam-based Nederland Line and the Rotterdam Lloyd of Rotterdam. All of the ships, such as the *Slamat*, *Sibajak* and *Indrapoera* (shown here), were named in reflection of their Eastern service. [*Indrapoera*: Built by the De Schelde Shipyards, Vlissingen, Holland, 1926. 10,772 gross tons; 499 feet long; 60 feet wide. Sulzer diesels geared to twin screw. Service speed 15 knots. 388 passengers (141 first class, 184 second class, 63 third class).]

ANGERS (opposite, top).

France's Messageries Maritimes handled the colonial trade from Marseilles out to Indochina. In ships such as the *Angers*, there was a constant relay of government personnel and their families, traders and workers, teachers and technicians, troops and their dependents and, on occasion, a tourist. [Built by Blohm & Voss Shipbuilders, Hamburg, Germany, 1907. 9,846 gross tons; 483 feet long; 53 feet wide. Quadruple expansion engines geared to twin screw. Service speed 15.5 knots. 373 passengers (151 first class, 142 second class, 80 troops).]

ANCHISES (opposite, bottom).

The Liverpool-based Blue Funnel Line was one of Britain's biggest shipping firms. Its ships were especially noted for their names, which were drawn from Greco-Roman mythology. Although most of the vessels were 12-passenger freighters, several others were given more extensive accommodations for the company services to the Middle East, Australia and the Orient.

Three sisters built in 1910–11 for the Australian run were the *Aeneas*, *Ascanius* and *Anchises*, all names drawn from Vergil's *Aeneid*. Unlike most ships on that run, these did not have vast immigrant quarters but only first-class spaces. [*Anchises*: Built by Workman, Clark & Company Limited, Belfast, Northern Ireland, 1911. 10,046 gross tons; 509 feet long; 60 feet wide. Steam triple expansion engines geared to twin screw. Service speed 14 knots. 288 first-class passengers.]

EMPRESS OF AUSTRALIA.

In the twenties, Canadian Pacific maintained the finest liner service across the Pacific. They offered an alternative to the Suez route to reach the Eastern portions of the British Empire. Using Vancouver as an eastern terminal, their famed Empress liners traveled to Hong Kong as well as Kobe and Yokohama in Japan and Shanghai in China. This service connected with the company's Atlantic liner fleet as well as its transcontinental rail operation. On the Pacific, there were four major liners—the *Empress of Russia, Empress of Canada, Empress of Australia* and *Empress of Asia*. With such ships, there was a sailing every two weeks from Vancouver.

The *Empress of Australia*, shown here, was just minutes away from departing from her Yokohama pier, on September 1, 1923, when the great earthquake struck that city. The ship was tossed and rattled violently but survived with little damage and was used as a most important medical and refugee center immediately after the calamity.

The first-class ballroom on board the *Empress of Australia* (*top*) reflects her earlier design intention as a German liner. In 1913, she had been ordered by the Hamburg-American Line as the *Tirpitz*. However, because of the results of the First World War, her original German shipbuilders completed her for the British, specifically for the Canadian Pacific Company, as reparations.

The ship's finest cabin accommodation (*middle*) was named in honor of the then very popular Prince of Wales, later the Duke of Windsor. The young prince had crossed aboard a Canadian Pacific liner, the *Empress of France*, in 1923. Much later, the spring of 1939, both the King and Queen of England used the Prince of Wales Suite as part of their accommodation on their goodwill visit to North America.

The first-class smoking room (*bottom*) was rather unusual in that it was uncarpeted. [Built by the Vulkan Shipyards, Stettin, Germany, 1913–20. 21,860 gross tons; 615 feet long; 75 feet wide. Steam turbines geared to twin screw. Service speed 16.5 knots. 1,513 passengers (404 first class, 165 second class, 270 third class, 674 steerage).]

OTRANTO (opposite, top).

On the England-Australia service, the chief competitor to the established P&O Lines was the Orient Line. All the Orient ships had the same initial letter as the line: *Orford, Orontes, Orama, Oronsay* and *Otranto* (shown here). They were among the finest ships on the "Down Under" trade, sailing between London, Gibraltar, Marseilles, Naples, the Suez Canal and Ceylon and then onward to Fremantle, Brisbane, Melbourne and Sydney. During the summers, ships such as the *Otranto* were often sent on cruises from London, usually to the Canaries, West Africa, the Mediterranean, the Norwegian fjords and the Baltic. [Built by Vickers-Armstrong Shipbuilders Limited, Barrow-in-Furness, England, 1925. 20,032 gross tons; 659 feet long; 75 feet wide. Steam turbines geared to twin screw. Service speed 20 knots. 1,686 passengers (572 first class, 1,114 third class).]

AORANGI (opposite, bottom).

Britain's *Aorangi* was the world's first large motorliner at her debut in 1924. Soon afterward, others followed with this new form of propulsion, an alternative to commonly used steam-turbine drive. As part of the Union Steamship Company of New Zealand, the *Aorangi* connected the Pacific Dominions: from Australia and New Zealand across to Western Canada. [Built by Fairfield Shipbuilding & Engineering Company, Glasgow, Scotland, 1924. 17,491 gross tons; 600 feet long; 72 feet wide. Sulzer diesels geared to quadruple screw. Service speed 17.5 knots. 947 passengers (436 first class, 284 second class, 227 third class).]

MATAROA (above).

The Shaw Savill Line offered connections between Britain and New Zealand. Two of their ships, the *Tamaroa* and the *Mataroa*, made regular sailings between London, Curaçao, the Panama Canal and then southward to Auckland and Wellington. [Built by Harland & Wolff Limited, Belfast, Northern Ireland, 1922. 12,341 gross tons; 519 feet long; 63 feet wide. Steam turbines geared to twin screw. Service speed 15 knots. 553 passengers (131 first class, 422 third class).]

LEVIATHAN.

As the twenties were drawing to a close, a new
period in ocean-liner history was beginning. A fresh
race was about to start between the maritime powers
of Europe—Britain, Germany, France and Italy—
with a new breed of superliners. These would be the
biggest, fastest and grandest yet seen. Also, shipboard decorations were rapidly changing, moving to
the more modern Art Deco stylings that were first
introduced on sea by the French liner *Ile de France* of
1927. Finally, the worldwide Depression would start
in the fall of 1929, adversely affecting shipping
throughout the world. Many of the ships covered in
these pages would sail half-full or nearly empty or,
worse still, be sent to the scrapheap prematurely. In
this rather poetic scene, the giant *Leviathan* departs
from New York on a moody winter afternoon. The
year is 1929. Soon she will be laid up, in the twilight
of her career.

BIBLIOGRAPHY

Armstrong, Warren: *Atlantic Highway*. London: George G. Harrap & Company, Limited, 1961.

Bonsor, N. R. P.: *North Atlantic Seaway*. Prescot, Lancashire: T. Stephenson & Sons, Limited, 1955.

Braynard, Frank O.: *Lives of the Liners*. New York: Cornell Maritime Press, 1947.

Braynard, Frank O.: *Leviathan: The Story of the World's Greatest Ship* (Volumes 1–5). New York: South Street Seaport, 1972–81.

Braynard, Frank O., & Miller, William H.: *Fifty Famous Liners*. Cambridge: Patrick Stephens, Limited, 1982.

Brinnin, John Malcolm: *The Sway of the Grand Saloon*. New York: Delacorte Press, 1971.

Cairis, Nicholas T.: *North Atlantic Passenger Liners Since 1900*. London: Ian Allan, Limited, 1972.

Coleman, Terry: *The Liners*. New York: G. P. Putnam's Sons, 1977.

Crowdy, Michael (editor): *Marine News* (journal, 1964–82). Kendal, Cumbria: World Ship Society.

Eisele, Peter (editor): *Steamboat Bill* (journal, 1966–82). New York: Steamship Historical Society of America.

Emmons, Frederick: *The Atlantic Liners: 1925–1970*. New York: Bonanza Books, 1972.

Gibbs, C. R. Vernon: *British Passenger Liners of the Five Oceans*. London: Putnam & Company, Limited, 1963.

Hitchcock, Raymond: *Attack on the Lusitania*. New York: St. Martin's Press, Inc., 1979.

Kludas, Arnold: *Great Passenger Ships of the World* (Volmes 1–5). Cambridge: Patrick Stephens, Limited, 1972–76.

Kludas, Arnold: *The Ships of the German-Africa Line*. Oldenburg: Verlag Gerhard Stalling AG, 1975.

Kludas, Arnold: *The Ships of the Hamburg-Süd 1871–1951*. Oldenburg: Verlag Gerhard Stalling AG, 1976.

Lord, Walter: *A Night to Remember*. New York: Henry Holt & Company, 1955.

MacLean, Donald: *Queen's Company*. London: Hutchinson & Company, Limited, 1965.

Marshall, Logan: *The Tragic Story of the Empress of Ireland*. Cambridge: Patrick Stephens, Limited, 1972.

Maxtone-Graham, John: *The Only Way to Cross*. New York: The Macmillan Company, 1972.

Miller, William H.: *The Great Luxury Liners 1927–1954*. New York: Dover Publications, Inc., 1981.

Miller, William H.: *Transatlantic Liners 1945–80*. Newton Abbot, Devon: David & Charles, Limited, 1981.

Morris, James: *The Great Port: A Passage Through New York*. New York: Harcourt, Brace & World, Inc., 1969.

Padfield, Peter: *Beneath the Houseflag of the P&O*. London: Hutchinson & Company, Limited, 1981.

Prager, Hans George: *Blohm & Voss: Ships and Machinery for the World*. Herford: Koehlers Verlagsgesellschaft, 1977.

Schaap, Dick, & Schaap, Dick: *A Bridge to the Seven Seas*. New York: Holland America Cruises, 1973.

Shaum, John H. & Flayhart, William H.: *Majesty At Sea*. Cambridge: Patrick Stephens, Limited, 1981.

Smith, Eugene W.: *Passenger Ships of the World Past and Present*. Boston: George H. Dean Company, 1963.

Turner, Robert D.: *The Pacific Empresses*. Victoria, British Columbia: Sono Nis Press, 1981.

van Herk, Cornelius: *The Ships of the Holland America Line*. Haarlem: Historische Boekhandel Erato, 1981.

Wall, Robert: *Ocean Liners*. New York: E. P. Dutton, 1977.

Witthoft, Hans Jurgen. *Hapag-Lloyd*. Herford: Koehlers Verlagsgesellschaft, 1979.

ALPHABETICAL LIST
OF SHIPS ILLUSTRATED

The pages listed are those containing the text references.